Looking at LIFE Differently

Minimising Tensions
Maximising Effectiveness

SWAMI SUKHABODHANANDA

Author of the best seller
Oh, Mind Relax Please!

Published by Prasanna Trust
51, Ground Floor, 16th Cross,
Between 6th & 8th Main, Malleswaram
Bangalore 560 003, India
E-Mail: prasannatrust@vsnl.com
www.swamisukhabodhananda.org

First Print	No. of copies	– 5,000
Second Print	No. of copies	– 5,000
Third Print	No. of copies	– 5,000
Fourth Prnt	No. of copies	– 5,000
Fifth Prnt	No. of copies	– 5,000

Cover Design : Suresh UT

Book Layout : Govardhan Kini K

Printed at
SUDHINDRA
Malleswaram, Bangalore 560 003, India

Price : Rs. 225/-
ISBN 81-901496-8-7

ABOUT THE AUTHOR

Swami Sukhabodhananda *has rich wisdom of both Oriental and Occidental teachings. In his enlightened 'presence' the book of life unfolds itself. His presence makes you feel that life is a bed of roses while difficulties help you build a heart of understanding. He guides you to evolve from a mere biological being to a spiritual being.*

His method of enquiry focuses on multi-dimensional aspects of life. He makes you experience inner bliss. He teaches the art of enjoying 'what is.' His overflowing presence gives you overwhelming clarity.

His several books have made many discover new ways of living life. He makes you realise that if one door closes another door opens. Life is an opening.

He is a regular invitee to various forums in India, USA, Canada, Germany and Australia. He has been addressing many gatherings at important Universities in India and abroad. Leading industrial houses invite him to conduct

'In-house workshops' for their executives. His self-development programs have benefited many in the corporate sectors including reputed institutions in banking, finance, industry and education.

He is the founder Chairman of Prasanna Trust. He is also the founder of the research wing of Prasanna Foundation, which focuses on the scientific aspects of meditation.

FOREWORD

This book facilitates the process of one's growing into a new being. The profane separates us and kills the soul. The profound initiates us into a miracle of life – the higher self. One has to let go of one's lower self and selfishness in order to be profound.

This book helps us drop illusions in life. Then one would not find death frightening but instead life would be ever inviting. By digesting the contents of the book, one's higher self would be one's living God. A new center would be created. A new order would be born. One would learn to swallow one's pride and never face indigestion in life.

This book provides you with a magical key to unlock the miracles of life. Thought and thinking keep the mind closed. No thought and non-thinking open your mind.

This book makes you look at life differently. It makes you understand that freedom is not an absence of bondage but in spite of it. You are free to be bound and hence bondage would not bind you. You discover an inner space, which cannot be bound by bondage. When 'you' don't exist, this miracle happens. The power of surrender becomes your inner breath.

You will be totally involved in the moment. This totality of the moment gives you a new birth. You start moving to your inner roots. You will not be foolish to be miserable but be wise to be ecstatic. You discover that all hopes are false. Hopes postpone your being happy. You start sharing your being in a new way.

You maximize your playfulness, trust and joy. You start respecting your heart and seeking ways to make yourself and others happy. Effectiveness will be a divine adventure and not proving to others that you are worthwhile.

An inner voice of silence will guide you like a loving mother. The greatest advice I received was when my mother told me to be like a butterfly. A butterfly does not disturb and burden others. It is colourful and light. It has the ability to draw pollen from the flowers, which others can't. Learn from others; don't disturb others but be light. Be colourful and life will lead you to a new way of living.

With blessings,

SWAMI SUKHABODHANANDA

FROM THE AUTHOR

I have always inspired myself that if I cannot be happy 'here and now,' I will never be happy anywhere. This book is an offering of my insights to create happiness in all walks of life. This is possible if one looks at life in a new way.... looking at life differently.

The superficial way of reading this book is through intellectual understanding. The deeper way is by feeling the insights of the narration. The deepest way is where these insights and parables light up your mind & heart in your hours of darkness and guide you like a spiritual friend.

Hence I invite you to read this book not just once, but many times over like a daily prayer... for prayer does not change the Lord but changes you.

By ingesting the essence of this book, you will realise what lies before you and behind you are nothing in comparison to what lies within you. Enlightenment is looking for spectacles that sit right on your nose. Enlightenment is always 'here and now,' never in the past or future. This book attempts to awaken you... like a wake up call.

To do what you like and like what you do is indeed a divine work. Work is an opportunity to find oneself. This book helps you in finding yourself in all walks of life... family, work, social, and spiritual zones. In the process, you will be grateful to the weeds of your mind. They ultimately help your practice of relaxation.

Being relaxed is wise. Begin with being wise and you will be relaxed. Being relaxed is a wise and an easy way to live life. When you are relaxed, you look at life differently.

Life, thus lived will bring forth the peace of a rose garden and light of the luminous Sun as a part of your being.

Let your growth bring the best seasons of your life. This is my humble prayer for you.

I specially thank P. R. Madhav for editing this book. My special thanks to Mrs. Devki Jaipuria for all her support. My salutation to my loving mother who is the source of my inspiration. My deepest gratitude, which cannot be expressed in words, goes out to all my Gurus. I offer this book to all my students who are like little lamps shining in the night, which the great Sun cannot do. This is my dream and I am sure you will join me in making it as your destination.

With blessings,

SWAMI SUKHABODHANANDA

Our heartfelt thanks to all enlightened masters & modern thinkers for their inspirational guidance.

CONTENTS

COMMITMENT AND EXCELLENCE IN LIFE

Commitment is the language of the wise; complaint is the language of the fools. Commitment is a responsibility and also includes accountability. In life, one should be responsible as well as accountable. Generally one takes responsibility without accountability; this weakens one's being.

Our weaknesses result in disappointment. Disappointment should be cremated and not garlanded. People derive a sadistic pleasure from disappointment. This is a primitive pleasure, like a grownup boy sucking his thumb. To cremate disappointment, one should strengthen one's strengths. The greatest strength comes from the energy of commitment and brings in excellence in all walks of life. Few people traverse the road of success without a puncture or two but it is commitment to excellence that takes them through.

Commitment is not being 'stuck,' but it is an integration of one's being. For example, if you are committed to honour your word, then the 'lower self' in you will discourage you to justify the failure in not keeping up your promise. If your energies are low, you will be sucked into its logic and reasoning. But if you follow the 'higher self,' the 'lower self' will be like a servant serving the master. Slowly the 'lower self' will be integrated with the higher. In such a state there will be integrity. Without integrity life is shallow.

We have, both - an actor and a thinker in us. Every time we lie, the thinker warns us that we are lying and the actor asks us to shut up and continue telling lies. In such a state, there is a split in our being – between the actor and the thinker. It is like riding a chariot with two horses, with the horses going in two different directions. Commitment creates integrity. In this state, it is easier to bring forth the excellence in our lives.

Observe nature and see how other beings are committed. For example, look at an eagle.

- From a range of 5 km, it focuses on its prey.

  Can we focus on our goals like an eagle?

- An eagle does not eat a dead prey.

  Can we learn not to live on dead information?

- If there is a storm, the eagle can glide on the strong breeze. It tests its wings and enjoys the storm and the challenges associated with it.

Can we enjoy difficulties and convert them into challenges?

- An eagle does not mix with other birds. It soars high on its own.

  Can we be part of an average crowd and still soar high on our strengths?

- An eagle tests before it trusts. Before mating, a female eagle tests its partner. It picks up a twig, flies high and as the male follows, it flies around to escape and finally drops the twig. Before the twig falls on the ground, the male catches the twig and gives it to the female. It repeats this act. If a male succeeds in catching the twig consistently, then it allows mating to take place.

Similarly, like an eagle, can we test before we trust?

- Eagles lay eggs on a cliff or at the edge of a high peak by making a nest of grass entwined with thorns. When the eggs hatch, the weight of the eaglets makes it uncomfortable as the thorns start pricking. Then the female pushes the eaglets out of the nest. As the eaglets are about to fall, the male picks them and brings them back to the nest. Meanwhile, the female removes the upper layer of grass, so that the eaglets rest directly on the thorns that prick them. The eaglets are yet to test their wings to fly. Now the male pushes the eaglets out of the nest. This process continues till such time that the eaglets are able to foresee the danger in falling and start using theirs wings. Slowly they realise their ability to use their wings and start flying.

Difficulties are like divine surgery. Do not resist difficulties. Nature expects us to use our heart and head to discover new and wiser skills to fly in life.

Observe the commitment of an eagle in bringing out excellence while choosing a partner first and parenting later. Bring similar commitment to all walks of life; be it at family, at work, in society or in your spiritual life.

Excellence happens when there is love to grow and contribute. Heart is like a musical instrument. Use it wisely.

Creativity occurs primarily through the power of intention. Intention is like sowing a seed in existence. Allow it to germinate. Allow the forces of nature to nurture life.

Commitment also involves dropping illusions. We do not see the world as it is. We see the world projected through our verbose minds. Minds are filled with thoughts, which are nothing but mere words. Words represent experiences. Words are also influenced by memory. Memory is of the past. From the past, we see the present. Hence we create illusions created by words, but we must filter them wisely.

The mind creates dreams. The self - awareness in you sees reality. Awareness without the arrogant 'I' is the 'higher self.' The mind with its illusions is the 'lower self.' Have the commitment to operate from the 'higher self.'

Through commitment, balance all walks of your life... family, work, social and spiritual. Creativity is to balance all walks of life. Creativity is just not creating something new always. Creativity brings excellence in one's life. It is a state of well-being. Well-being creates completion. When one is complete, one is alive and vibrant in all walks of life.

A teacher advised, 'Let this not happen to you all.'

First, I was dying to finish high school with an 'A' grade.

Then, I was dying to enter the best college.

Then, I was dying to finish college.

Then, I was dying to get a good job.

Then, I was dying to get married.

Then, I was dying to have children.

Then, I was dying to see my children study well.

Then, I was dying to retire.

Then, all of a sudden I got this insight that I have forgotten to live.

CONTEXT

SHAPES THE EXPERIENCE

You always state in your workshops that the context of an experience shapes the experience and hence people find it difficult to experience an experience. Can you please unfold further?

To experience an experience, one has to be present to an experience. If one is present in 'what is,' one will realise how one's past starts interfering with the present experience.

Reflect on this.

A passenger tapped the cab driver to ask a question. The cab driver lost control of the cab, nearly hit another car, missed another truck, went off the road, into a kerb and stopped inches from a shop. For a minute there was silence. 'You scared me to death,' the driver screamed.

The passenger apologized and said, 'I did not know that gently tapping your back could create such a panic.'

The driver replied, 'Sorry. It is not your mistake. Today is my first day as a cab driver. For the last ten years I have been ferrying dead bodies in a van.'

Can you see how his past shaped the present?

Our experiences are influenced by the past. So one has to be conscious and aware. One has to be present in 'what is' and not allow the past to shape the present. To be present in every moment is very important.

Why is it that most of us choose the wrong path and be sad?

When you are unhappy, there is a pay-off. People give you sympathy. When you are happy, you have to pay a price .... people feel jealous of you. So unhappiness has a deceptive gain in you getting sympathy from people around and in misleading you into believing that sympathy is equal to love. So first one has to renounce this myth.

When you get sympathy you get a lot of attention and attention is delicious food for the ego.

Since childhood you play this racket of getting attention. As you grow up this game continues. Have you seen beautiful girls? They tempt men and when a man falls for them, they push him aside and thus feel strong. This is called the 'kiss me off racket.' Men also use anger as a racket to protect their inner wound. Anger in such a case becomes a defence mechanism.

Rackets are manipulative games to seek attention. They are types of mental sickness. One's psychological immune system becomes weak. Hence, one is prone to the path of wrong, like when one's body's immune system is weak, one is prone to an infection.

Does one choose to be miserable in this mental game?

Yes. This has become a habit. Habit becomes a pattern. Then the pattern takes control of you. For example the victim pattern - being a victim invokes sympathy from others. So your misery becomes an investment. Then slowly it becomes a pattern. Then without your awareness, you will feel victimised. When some one smiles at you, you suspect that he has some motives and if some one does not smile at you, then you feel he hates you. This pattern attracts victimising situations too. So a miserable person attracts miserable people and they support each other's energies. This happens unconsciously and mechanically. One has to become aware of this energy drainer.

Become aware. Each time you are miserable, it is your choice. This is your game. You have some hidden agenda. If you see the foolishness of the hidden agenda, then you will drop it. It is like being tempted to eat excess sweets, but the moment you know it is harmful, you will not be tempted to eat them.

By this mental game I gain attention. Is this the food for the ego? Is my ego built on this foundation?

Yes. This is the foundation. Ego is built on hopes. Ego always lives in the past and the future. It is a storehouse of dreams. If you live in the present, there is no past or future. If you just sit in front of a stream and be present in 'what is,' there is no past or future. Ego can never exist in the present. Many people visit religious centres and holy masters not for enlightenment, but with hidden expectations that they want to fulfil. Enlightenment is in the present. It cannot be in the future. Hence, be in the present and see the magic of life.

Why is it so difficult to drop the ego?

The perception of 'easy' or 'difficult' depends on your state of being. Generally it is difficult as our whole life's journey hinges on ego trips. We want to be rich Why? Not for fulfilling our basic needs. Ego wants us to be richer than others. We want power. Not for contribution but because we want to feel better than others. We want to be different. Ego continues to seek more of name, fame, money, prestige and sometimes religiousness.

Running after the ego's wants is like chasing your own shadow. By understanding this, life will be liberating.

Our sufferings have come through our ego and our pleasures have also come through our ego. Pleasures are deceptive. Our sufferings are an illusion. Learn to be a witness to your pleasures. You will see a self that is above joy and sorrow. In fact, you can see and experience a self that is above joy and sorrow. More than an experience, it is an experience-less experience.

What do you mean when you say the real master is 'within?' It is so frustrating that when we have questions, we can't consult you. Is there a way out?

In each one of us there is a master and a student. The student is the surface and the master is your inner depth. The external master introduces you to the real master within you. In order to discover the inner master, you should stop living on the surface. Even when you meet an external master, you see him mainly as the body as you operate from the body … the 'lower self.' The external master is more a 'presence.' He is silence, love and bliss. Be meditative and realise that he is more than a body.

Similarly, you are a 'presence.' You are silence, from which thoughts and feelings emerge. Thoughts are your surface but you are the inner space of silence.

Buddha, Krishna and Jesus can still be communicated to, if only you are more meditative. Their 'presence' is never destroyed. Lord Krishna in the Gita says, 'They are fools who consider me to be only the body.' All great masters can be connected to, if you are more meditative. You need not be frustrated if you can't meet your master. Be in silence. Ask your question in that space of silence and you get an answer not from the mind but from the beyond. You have to experience this. This is not a matter of logic, it is a matter of experience.

How can I be more meditative in all walks of life?

If you are bathing, feel the blessings of God in the form of water. While walking, feel the blessings of God in the form of earth. Feel the breeze as God nourishing you. Even inert objects have life. Give love and be aware always. Life without love is a graveyard. Life with love is God.

THE ART OF WISE LIVING

A man went to a butcher's shop and asked for the best meat available. 'We keep only the best meat here,' replied the butcher. This enlightened the man as he realised that every moment is the best moment.

Every moment is the best moment. Can we treat every moment as the best moment? The art of wise living is to be present in the present as a present. Most of us do not experience an experience. We are busy butchering the experience from our concepts of good and bad, right and wrong; thereby missing the experience altogether. To be open to an experience is to chew and munch on that experience. In this space, experience guides you mysteriously.

What do you mean, when you term 'experience an experience?'

A student asked the master 'What was your experience before and after enlightenment?'

The master replied, 'Before enlightenment I used to wake up, bathe, eat, chop wood and sleep at night. After enlightenment, I did the same,' he continued.

'The only difference being, previously when I was doing similar chores, my mind used to be in the past or future. After enlightenment, when I eat - I eat, when I bathe - I bathe and hence I live in the present.'

To experience an experience is to be present in that experience. Very often our mind judges an experience on the basis of our likes and dislikes. So the energy of our likes and dislikes is superimposed on that experience. It is similar to a movie projected on the screen and the screen not being visible.

Is it ever possible to free us from likes and dislikes?

Do we have likes and dislikes or do likes and dislikes have us? As unconscious beings, likes and dislikes control our lives. Conscious beings are masters of likes and dislikes. When likes and dislikes are under your control, they will serve you and in such a state, you are not messed up. Likes and dislikes are not the problem. However, do they control your life, or are you controlling them, is the real question.

You talk about living in the present. What then is the usefulness of the past and the future?

It is wrong to say that we have to live only in the present. One needs to consider time as past, present and future. Some people are past oriented – mostly they operate from the past. Some are future oriented – mostly they operate from the future and some are present oriented – mostly operating from the present. To be wise, involves balancing time... when required you have to take reference from the past or consider the future. Hence balancing time is very essential.

Would you please elaborate on balancing time?

Do not reject the past or future. Also do not live only in the past or future. Learn from the past, enjoy the present and plan for the future. Be present in the past and thereby learn from the past, be present in the future, thereby plan for the future. Being alive in the present, you will enjoy the present. It is said that, one of the reasons Hitler lost the war was because he did not learn from history. He attacked Russia in winter. Had he learnt from history, he would have known that Napoleon had lost many of his men by attacking Russia in winter.

One can learn from the past as well as from the future taking care not to be imprisoned by both. Similarly, while planning for the future, do not lose the present and miss the wisdom of the past or the opportunities in the future. Hence, one needs to be balanced with reference to time.

Can you elaborate on time management?

- Decide on your priorities in life.
- Prioritise your priorities.

- Establish your peak performance time.....during a day.
- Monitor your low performance time.
- Do any important task at your peak performance time.
- Do any less important task at your low performance time.
- Identify your time wasters.
- Learn to delegate work.
- Enjoy your work and you will find there is a lot of time.
- Review your priorities from time to time.
- Be with people who are good at time management.

Can you explain the mystery of time?

Time consists of the past, the present, and the future. Just as the past was the present at one point of time, the future will also be the present at another point of time. So be present in the past and also be present in the future. Therefore, the present is more real.

What defines the present?

One hour. One hour has sixty minutes. A minute has sixty seconds. Further, break down the second and still further, the present will lose itself into 'is-ness.'

Time will melt into timelessness. Use time to go beyond time.

Why should one go beyond time?

Within us, there is a dimension of time and beyond time. We live in two worlds, a world of the mind, which is in time and a world beyond the mind that is timelessness. When we are in sleep or in *samadhi*, we go beyond mind and experience timelessness. One should have the wisdom to use the mind and the wisdom to go beyond the mind.

In a state of deep joy, we are beyond our minds.

What do you mean by 'The wisdom to use the mind?'

Mind is a bundle of thoughts. More than heart attacks, we suffer from thought attacks.

When thoughts attack us, we become victims of thoughts. It is like employing a servant and being thrashed by him. You should be the master of the mind rather than the mind being your master. You should use the mind rather than let the mind use you. The very intention to be the master of the mind will give you the wisdom of how to use the mind.

I am still not clear on the expression, 'The wisdom to use the mind.'

OK. Look at it from this angle. People complain about their wives dominating them, their bosses dominating them. However, if you closely observe, it is our own mind that dominates our lives. Just as in the case of Obsessive Compulsive Behaviour, wherein one washes hands continuously even when not required; in a similar manner there are compulsive thoughts. Mind constantly chatters. The chattering mind dominates us. When compulsive thoughts exist, we become slaves to them. Once you learn to be calm, you are in control. When required, use thoughts; when not, just be empty.

Why should one be calm and go beyond mind?

Generally we are dominated by thoughts ... compulsive thoughts. When the mind is noisy, we feel burdened. There is a voice of the mind and also there is a voice of the soul. The voice of the soul is silence. We do not experience silence, as our mind is noisy. The voice of the soul is nourishing, whereas the voice of the noisy mind is perishing. In order to hear the voice of the soul, one should put an effort to end the noisy mind.

Why do people consume drugs like LSD....?

A noisy and pushy mind leads one to a state of unhappiness. It constantly bullies and dominates us. We have become slaves to it; we want to escape from it. Some use mind-blocking or mind-altering drugs such as heroin, ecstasy or LSD. The temporary illusion of calming the mind takes away the stresses and we feel unburdened and relaxed. This momentary relief of noise and pressure leads to repeated use of drugs.

When we get addicted to drugs, our body and mind become their slaves again.

However, there is another way to achieve the tranquillity we need. A far healthier method is Meditation through which our bodies and minds remain in total mastery.

One day a man came to Mullah Nazarudin and said, 'Do something but rid me of my stomach ache.' Mullah took a stone and smashed the man's leg. The man yelled in pain and screamed, 'Why did you do that?'

Mullah replied, 'Now you don't have stomach ache, do you?'

What a foolish way to escape from pain. To get rid of one problem we enter into another. Similarly, to get rid of the burden of a noisy mind people get into drugs and suffer.

The Art of Being Happy

What constitutes being happy?

Being happy involves destroying the 'hurt body.' We are not conscious as to how we create a hurt body. Every thought creates energy - substance. This substance created by thought, is subtle and can be negative or positive. If a thought is negative, then the substance created by the thought grows and builds up. This results in creation of a subtle hurt body. This hurt body starts majoring on minor things and looks at the world independently. Thus, we do not see and think through our eyes and minds only, but we see and think through the eyes of the hurt body also. The secret of happiness lies in destroying the hurt body by creating a bliss body.

How is this bliss body created?

Every thought creates energy. Entertain happy thoughts and feelings, thereby creating happy energies. This happy energy creates a bliss body and then your life will be happy.

Isn't this just positive thinking?

Initiate positive thinking and let it progressively transform into wise thinking; for which a guru's guidance is needed. When thinking happens through a wise blend of both male and female energies, such thinking is referred to as wise thinking. It involves your seeing 'what is' as is, and 'what is not' as is not. Wise thinking makes you see a possibility of what can be, whereas positive thinking makes you see what can be but negates 'what is.'

The next stage is going beyond thoughts. Learn to see yourself beyond thoughts. Between thoughts, there is silence; there is a gap that is beyond thoughts. Once you see this gap - silence, there exists bliss. This bliss is not born out of thought and so cannot be destroyed by thought. This is called the bliss body of an enlightened being. Silence makes you discover this bliss body.

What you mean by both 'male and female energies?'

We are products of our parents and hence, there exist both male and female energies in us. Traits of the male energy include achievement, assertiveness … and those of the female energy include acceptance, passiveness ….. Some people are very assertive, but there is no energy of acceptance in them, resulting in an imbalance of energies. The thinking of such an imbalanced person is distorted. A man may possess more of female energy and vice versa. Hence, a proper balance of these two energies is necessary.

Is there a special discipline of balancing the male and the female energies?

If female energy is dominant in a person, such a person needs to be trained in an aggressive form of martial arts like karate or judo and if male energy is dominant in a person, such a person needs to be trained in gentle forms of energy techniques like taichi, gardening or music to counterbalance such energies. In yoga, there are certain postures that enhance the male or the female energies. Hence, a guru would be best placed to guide you wisely.

Mind is meant to think but not to be kept empty; can you please elaborate on this statement?

When required, think. If thinking happens without your awareness, it is compulsive and hence mechanical. Mechanical thinking is no thinking. To energise your thinking, keep your mind calm and empty. It is a known fact that many scientists think deeply on a subject, go to sleep and in the middle of the night often find answers mysteriously. Resting the mind energizes it. Waking up after a good restful sleep, you feel refreshed. Learn the art of being empty and in this emptiness when you start thinking, your thinking will have the power and vitality.

Can you narrate a story to inspire us?

In the house of a famous swordsman named Shoken, there lived a large rat that was fomenting trouble. The swordsman brought in a female cat to kill the rat. With pride, the cat arrived at the house of the swordsman. The cat went into the room and saw the rat. Surprisingly, the rat attacked the cat. Shamefully the cat had to leave the house without being able to catch the rat.

The swordsman later invited a male cat since the female cat had failed in its attempt to catch the rat. In similar fashion as the female cat, the rat attacked the male cat. The male cat too left the room unsuccessfully. Puzzled by this turn of events, the cats called for a conference to discuss the matter. Amongst them, a wise old female cat volunteered to catch the rat.

The swordsman was surprised to see the old cat. The old cat went into the room and saw the large rat. Both of them had an eye contact. The old cat approached the rat, took it in her mouth, and quietly left the room. The other cats asked the old cat to divulge the secret of her success.

The old cat replied, 'All of you have used techniques to catch the rat and the rat had better techniques to counter you. Whereas, I went with emptiness. When I was void, I had no form, no desire to attack. When one has no form and desire, then one is not a threat to an other. Then a great energy .... the divine energy flows through us. When there is 'I,' there is a form and one's form is a threat to the other form. When there is no 'I,' there is no threat to the other, and hence no enmity. I allowed existence to decide who to catch whom? That was the secret of my success.'

The great swordsman bowed down to the old female cat and said, 'You are speaking Zen. I have the theory and you have the practise.'

You mean to say that when there is no 'I' - the Ego, divine intelligence will flow?

Yes. Our ego - the 'I' is like dust in the eyes. When there is dust in the eyes, the whole universe appears to be chaos. Ego is the dust in the eyes of consciousness. Be empty, surrender your ego and allow divine intelligence to flow. The old female cat was empty and allowed the cosmic intelligence to flow. In such a state of surrender either a rat or a cat would win. Such surrender requires great commitment. Allow this cosmic intelligence to flow through you.

Goodness
THE FOOD FOR THE SOUL

In the present times, people are more inclined towards glamour than goodness. Media gives glamour the utmost importance; it has become a status symbol. People seem to be brainwashed into believing that glamour is equal to happiness. If one is glamorous, then one will be happy… is the false notion they carry. The media strongly and cunningly sows this myth. The power of this myth is ruling the present world.

Why does glamour have more appeal than goodness?

There are three traits in human consciousness. Looking good, feeling good and being good. The most important of these traits is 'being-good.' Many people value 'feeling-good.' However, if 'feeling-good' is not anchored on being good, then people get into drugs …. Drugs temporarily make you feel good, but are not good for your well-being.

People also value looking good more. Impressing another is of primary importance. For them, looking good, physically and psychologically is more important than feeling good and being good. There is nothing wrong in looking good, as long as it is based on being good. More often, people want their image to be appreciated to feed their ego. Glamour is food for the ego; it decorates your 'looking-good' pattern. Hence, glamour is of a greater appeal.

Why is 'Looking-good' wrong?

It is not a question of right or wrong. There exists a deeper meaning to it.

Reflect on this real incident.

A young girl from an orthodox Indian family became a widow at the age of 20. She expressed to me in one of my workshops that she was feeling lonely. I asked her why she could not remarry. She replied that she came from an orthodox family and feared what people would say if she were to get married again. I asked her as to what people were talking about her right then. She replied that they felt that she was a good woman. However, I asked her, if she was feeling-good. In the eyes' of the people, she was looking-good but was not feeling-good.

People sacrifice 'feeling-good' and 'being-good' for the sake of 'looking-good.' By not remarrying, she was not being-good to herself. When looking-good is not based on being-good, then life becomes a mess.

The world runs on the illusion of looking-good. If you do not look good, you will not survive this rat race, little realising that even if you win, you continue to be a rat. Are people happy in spite of being successful? Why is it that many successful people are still miserable? The reason being that they do not know the art of being happy. A study done on happy people showed that happy people were good finders. They always seek and find something good even in the bad.

Use the image of looking-good but do not be used by the image of looking-good. Just as you wear a dress, you are not the dress; so you are not the image. To be happy, be free from any image of yourself. Be empty of image, empty of thoughts, empty of conclusions. This inner emptiness is joy. This is a new way of looking.

Why should I be a good individual as being good involves more problems?

In my workshops, I ask people, if you are going to die within an hour, what would you want other people to talk about you? People throughout the world want only good things to be spoken of them. Nobody wants others to talk ill of them. It is thus clear that we are all seeking goodness.

Being a good individual requires facing problems. In fact, being a bad individual also involves facing problems. Problems are a part of life; hence do not be against them. Train your mind to enjoy problems. Just as you go to a gym and enjoy the work-out in spite of sweating. Similarly, train your mind to enjoy problems. Problems at times make a powerful individual of you.

Will you please narrate a story?

Long ago in Persia, there lived a king, who was interested in seeking answers to his spiritual questions but could not get the right answers. He went and met a great mystic called Zarathustra and asked him for words of wisdom. Instead of giving the king words of wisdom, Zarathustra gave him wheat seeds. The king felt insulted, threw the seeds and went away. He continued on his pursuit of acquiring more wealth. At the fag end of his life, he felt he had given away his life for wealth and it would not protect him at the time of his death. He pondered whether he had invested his life wrongly.

He once again sent word to the great mystic Zarathustra to bestow upon him his words of wisdom. Again, the mystic presented wheat seeds to the king. The king felt he was not mature enough to understand Zarathustra's message and kept the seeds in his prayer room.

Later, the king called a philosopher from India to teach and guide him. The philosopher told the king that the real purpose of his coming was not to teach the king, but to meet the mystic Zarathustra. The king showed the philosopher the seeds sent by the mystic.

Looking at the seeds, the philosopher cried aloud, 'What words of wisdom! what seeds of wisdom!

what a great teaching!' The king pleaded with the philosopher to elaborate. The philosopher replied, 'The seeds appear to be finite, but they have infinite capacity to grow. From a seed, a tree and from a tree again a seed and so on. In the same way, we appear to be finite like this seed, but deep within we have infinite capacity to grow.

Secondly, unless the seed is willing to give up its seed-hood, it cannot grow. Similarly, unless we are willing to bury our past we cannot grow to a new future. The art of wise living is the art of dying.

Finally, when you plant seeds in the ground, invisible forces like water, heat, air … will help the seed sprout. One should have trust. In life too, we should trust goodness and the invisible forces would help us get enlightened.'

Both the king and the philosopher met Zarathustra. He welcomed them but did not teach them anything. He asked them to observe him and learn. While they were gardening in the company of the great mystic, they realized that any species survives only if it is organic. If a seed is unwilling to multiply, the species will die. Likewise, goodness and wisdom should also be organic. Learn to spread this goodness and wisdom.

Thank you for this great message. Is there anything more?

Remember, you are like a seed. The periphery is finite, but deep within, you are an infinite possibility.

Just as a seed has to be organic in order to survive, be organic in spreading goodness. You are a seed and you should be a wise gardener. Even in the materialistic world, you are a possibility. To succeed in this world be organic. People love to trust a good individual rather than a bad one. Therefore, apply this technique to your spiritual and materialistic success.

What should be the purpose of one's life?

Learn to be successful and satisfied in life. Success is getting what you like and satisfaction is liking what you get. Life should be a balance of both success and satisfaction.

Work for success and let work be fun, do not work for fun. By working for success, you fulfil your accomplishment needs. With more of success that you achieve, be grateful and thankful so that your success will not lead you to be egoistic. Remember, ego is Edging God Out.

To be satisfied involves being at peace with 'what is.' Do not create a conflict with 'what is.' Be in harmony with it. Learn to see elegance in imperfection; to see beauty in 'what is' and not in what it should be. You will then be satisfied.

Should we not drop our desires in order to be happy?

Spiritual teachers tell us to drop desires, whereas materialistic people ask us to increase desires. In my opinion, both are wrong. Make desires sacred, by which you transcend them. Desires have two ends like a pole. One end is the object of desire. Learn to enjoy the object and do good to the world. The other end of the desire is you. In the process of doing good to the world, are you growing in silence, love, peacefulness and gratefulness? If so, then you are growing. By working on both the ends, you make your desires sacred and transcend them. Thus, desire is a problem only if you have not made it sacred.

Does growth involve seeing both the ends?

Yes, horizontal growth occurs in the world of objects. Enjoy and do good. Acquire wealth out of goodness. Vertical growth involves you being more loving, kind, silent, and grateful, thereby providing you with real happiness. Horizontal growth only provides you with pleasures. There is a remarkable difference between pleasure and happiness. Be aware of this distinction.

The Joy of Looking

There are two types of looking. You can look at the world through thoughts; you can look at the world without thoughts, from a 'pure being.' When you look at the world through thoughts, then, you should be aware of the subtle pollution that exists. Thoughts come from memory and memory is the representation of an experience of the past. So from the past you see the present. Hence, pollution occurs.

Is it not natural that we look at the world through thoughts?

The moment you say, it is natural, the possibility of a higher perception does not exist. You can say, ordinarily, you look through thoughts. However, there is an extra-ordinary way of looking at life. Have you not observed many physically challenged people doing extra-ordinary things in life? That is exactly what I am inviting you to explore.

Should we therefore avoid thoughts?

No. There is a perception that happens through thoughts and there is a perception that can happen from a pure being or consciousness. Just be well versed in both these perceptions. Then you would be able to choose wisely. If you have learnt the art of looking from your being, then as required, you will see through your thoughts. As a result, you have the thoughts and the thoughts do not have you. You will notice that thoughts are not controlled by memory, but memory will guide your thoughts. Generally memory imprisons thoughts. This possibility happens if you have learnt not to be totally dependent on your thoughts.

Is there a special technique or meditation that you would advise us so as to experience a state beyond thoughts?

Just see yourself like bamboo. Bamboo is hollow inside like a flute. Whenever you are free, see yourself as an empty flute or bamboo. Your body is just like a flute empty within. Let your thoughts come and go, but do not identify with them, just be a witness. Be a passive witness and not an active witness to your thoughts. When you see a girl passing by, you participate with that perception actively; this is not the witness that I refer to but be a passive witness .... like when a dry leaf falls, you just observe. Passive looking is meditation.

Be like an empty flute. Passively observe the thoughts that come by. By practising being empty, there would be no barrier for the divine to enter you. This is a wonderful form of meditation. Meditate on nothingness. You are nothing and in that nothingness, you will experience fullness.

Why does the mind always revel in memory?

This happens because you have not trained yourself in the art of looking.

Buddha was once asked, 'Are you from heaven?'

'No,' replied Buddha.

'Are you a celestial being?'

'No,' said Buddha.

'Are you a human being?'

'No,' was his reply.

'Then who are you?' asked the man.

'I am a mirror of consciousness reflecting whatever is,' was Buddha's message.

This is a wonderful message. Can our mind be like a mirror just reflecting whatever is? Most often, our mind is like a camera; it goes on storing images. Then at the time of death, our soul cannot easily leave the body as our memories create attachments.

Just practise being a mirror, reflect what is in the present, do not unnecessarily burden your mind, by carrying memories of the past. Just be a pure mirror. Practise this and see the miracle happening in your life. You will be as light as a feather.

The mother of all problems is an untrained mind. An unhappy mind, in heaven, will create hell and a happy mind in hell, will create heaven. Heaven and hell are states of mind. One can live in the most wonderful house and still experience hell. Why does this happen? This happens because one has not trained one's mind. Mind is like an elephant, if trained it can be very useful but an untrained elephant is hell in motion.

Can you elaborate on the mind and its management?

One needs to -

- Understand the mind
- Transform the mind
- Transcend the mind.

Firstly, when you try to understand the mind, you will realise that the mind is not a static object, but a process. Mind is a crowd of thoughts that come and go. It is not static, but dynamic. This process of thoughts creates an illusion. We suffer because of this illusion. In fact, there is no such thing as the mind; it is only the thoughts that exist.

Secondly, you can transform the mind, if you can see the gaps between thoughts. Learn to see the gaps between thoughts. There is profundity hidden in these gaps. Once you learn to be in these gaps between thoughts, you will be able to manage the thoughts very easily. You will notice that the thoughts are an extension of your values. If you relish alcohol, you will have thoughts of alcohol. If you change your values, your thoughts will automatically change. However, first learn to be in the gaps ..... in the silence between the thoughts.

Finally, once the mind is pure, then you can transcend thoughts. Just practise being a witness to the thoughts but do not identify with them.

Change your values and your thoughts will change. How do we achieve this change?

Value is that which you give importance to. You give importance to something, with the feeling that you will benefit from it. If you value alcohol, what is it that you are going to benefit or lose? Be aware of the price that you are paying and the payoff that you would receive from it. The more you consume alcohol, the more you lose not only your health but also your wealth. What then is the purpose of consuming alcohol? Is it to attain relaxation?

Instead, teach yourself healthy ways in which you can relax. Thus, apply the price and the pay off technique and train your mind to change your values.

How do we transcend the mind?

The mind is a process. Mind is nothing but thoughts. When thoughts come, do not identify with them. See them as 'seen' and you are the 'seer.' The seer is not the seen. A car is seen and you are the seer and hence you are not a car. Similarly, thoughts are seen and you are the seer and hence you are not the thoughts. Do not identify with your thoughts. In addition, whenever you are free, do not unnecessarily verbalise an experience; this will lead you to go beyond thoughts.

What do you mean by 'do not word' an experience?

For example, while you are bathing, do not mentally go on talking. Just experience the experience of bathing. Be mentally void. The joy of being without words is a new taste bud that one needs to develop.

If you are mentally wording every experience, then you miss seeing 'what is.' A constant mental vomiting occurs. So learn to be without words. When required use mental words, when not required be like an empty flute. This will teach you to transcend your mind.

What occurs when you transcend the mind?

There is an unexplained joy. In deep sleep, you are happy. Not all the joy of external happiness put together is equal to the joy of sleep. If you were given a choice between no sleep and being the richest man in the world, what would you prefer? The choice is obvious. You may have all the wealth but if there is no sleep, you are in a rich hell. In sleep, you are beyond the mind.

When you transcend thoughts, you will realize that you are the host and your thoughts are like guests. You are the sky and the thoughts are like clouds. This experiential understanding is liberating.

How does this help in relationships?

Most problems of married couples exist because their minds are constantly churning compulsive thoughts. Thoughts are often the expression of memory. Memory is the representation of a past experience and then the past will interfere with the present. So when couples fail to see the partners afresh, they see from a past experience. The past had a different reality then and the present has a different reality now. If you can keep your mind empty, then compulsive thoughts and conclusions will not dominate your relationships. With such an inner freedom, you will relate to your partner more freely and wisely.

What about the differences in relationships?

When your mind is calm and empty, you will have the wisdom to realize that it is OK to have differences. When the mind says, it is not OK to have differences then there is stress. However, if you say it is OK to have differences, then you will be at peace with differences. You will see beauty in differences. You will not be a victim of your concept of beauty. You will see beauty in 'what is.'

PILLARS TO THE SKY

A young boy often looked up at the sky, fearing that the sky might fall any time, as it had no pillars to hold it. He ran into the forest, with the hope, that the trees would act as pillars to the sky and save him from being crushed if it fell.

In the forest, he came across a monk and asked him, 'Are you not afraid that the sky may fall as there are no pillars supporting the sky?'

The monk replied, 'There are pillars supporting the sky, but you need special eyes to see them.'

'How do I possess those special eyes?' asked the boy.

The monk's suggestion to the boy was to go to the village and arrogantly demand food. If villagers gave food with a difference, then he was to come and report to the monk.

The boy went to many houses, arrogantly seeking food. Most people refused to oblige him. Surprisingly, in one house, a woman came and begged his pardon for the delay in giving him food as she was feeding her baby. When this incident was reported to the monk, he said, 'This act of goodness of the woman, is one of the pillars supporting the sky.'

Every good act is a pillar propping the sky. It is not visible but it exists. If life comes from such belief, then you get strength from an unknown source.

Is goodness the only way of life? Many people are good but they are not successful... has goodness failed?

Goodness should be the substratum on which life is built. Being good is important, but being good alone does not lead to success. To be successful, one should also be smart. People think that only working hard is going to make them successful. This is a false belief. It is not only working hard but also working smart that make us successful. Goodness gives us spiritual strength, but one has to be smart in life... another variable that one needs to develop.

How do we develop smartness in life?

Being in the company of smart people one learns to develop smartness in life. One of the qualities of successful people is being skilful with others. They are good in their people skills. They know how to motivate people and get motivated by them in turn.

They know the art of accepting people and gracefully rejecting them when required, to present their point of view and not 'poke' their point of view. Successful people know how and when to praise others. They also know the art of sandwiching criticism between praises. They have a commitment to excel and treat failures as fertilizers to success. They are not like oak trees in flowerpots!

What is wrong if I am smart but devoid of goodness? I want to be successful by any means. We see this happening in the corporate world today. Is this philosophy wrong?

Understand that as you sow, so you reap.

A girl quarrels with her mother and goes to the forest behind her house. She vents out her anger yelling loudly, 'I hate you, I hate you.'

She is shocked to hear a voice 'I hate you, I hate you.' She runs to her mother and confides that some one was saying that she hates her. Mother knowing it was only an echo, lovingly tells her daughter, "Go back and tell her ' I love you' and then see what happens."

Life works on this echo principle.

If you are successful without goodness, you will not be in a position to enjoy the joy of your success. Your mind will be like a pot with a hole; any amount of water of success will leak through the hole.

Goodness makes the pot of your mind contain the joys of your success.

The greed to be somebody and the fear of being nobody is the greatest stress that people go through today. This is because they lack the foundation of goodness.

Can goodness help me in my business?

If you have two business partners, one who you feel is good and the other not so good, you will obviously choose the partner who is good. Criminals too, like their followers to be loyal to them. An ideal combination would be a good and a smart person.

In the 'presence' of a good individual, you will not feel threatened. You will feel safe and belonged. A value based business is much needed.

Is relationship based on pleasure? Does pleasure play an important role in a relationship. Is not goodness a binding factor in having fun in life?

The relationship between a man and a woman has the ingredient of pleasure. Nevertheless, there are different levels of pleasure. A child sucking his thumb is one form of pleasure, but when the child becomes an adult and if he continues sucking his thumb, then he is trapped in primitive pleasures. Hence, carefully observe the different levels of pleasure.

There is a pleasure of the body. There is a pleasure of belonging, a pleasure of being loyal, of being good. There is also a pleasure of contributing...

Goodness is the highest form of pleasure. In that pleasure, include all the other pleasures. The banks of the river do not bind the river. Similarly, discipline of goodness harnesses life and does not bind it. Reflect on this deeply.

What about goodness in our personal life, how does it contribute?

Goodness gives you integrity. Integrity unites you and lack of it breaks you.

How do you deal with bad people at work or in the society?

Learn to accept that the world is like a forest where you will come across all types of animals. You have to be alert, accepting and be able to protect yourself. Every person's soul is on a journey. Learn to accept it. Also, learn to empower them ... more by your 'presence' than by your words.

Words are shallow for those who are too much in the mind. They will be lost in words. If you have learnt to go beyond the mind, then your 'presence' will have magic. The energies of your heart and your being will flow. Invisible ripples of your consciousness will start communicating to the other. It is said that when Lord Buddha walked, flowers not in season bloomed because his consciousness was very powerful.

Why should I learn to accept a bad person?

There is very little choice that you have other than in accepting. Even if you reject him, he will still exist in this cosmos. When I say accept, I do not mean that you agree with him but be at peace with him. Learn to see elegance in imperfection. Understand that his being bad is communicating something to you. Existence is teaching you how not to be like him, through him. Hence, be grateful to him for in his badness lies a lesson for you to learn, how bad it is to be bad.

What do I do if my mother-in-law is bad? She constantly quarrels with me, uses harsh words but fortunately, she does not live with me.

When people use harsh words, it means that they are only expressing their hurt. If you do not accept those words, they will not hurt you. Gandhiji once said that nobody could take away your self-respect until you give it away. No one can hurt you until you give permission to be hurt. This is a great opportunity for you to practise of not getting hurt. Hurt or upset, whether justified or not, is self-damaging.

If your mother-in-law screams at you, do not listen from your mind, just listen to her from emptiness.

Look at her compassionately... she may be fighting a hard battle that we know nothing about, so be kind.

Learn to practise the technique of being an empty bamboo. Alternately, visualise that you are a transparent being. Let her words pass through you. When a stone is thrown in space it just passes but if there is a wall then there is a clash. Ego is like a wall on which the word clashes. Practise being empty.

Be grateful to your mother-in-law for giving you the opportunity to practise kindness. Convert the difference into a salvation point.

What you say appears to be nice but is it easy to practise?

It may not be easy but enjoy practising hard things in life. However, the fact is that it is easy to practise. Our ego makes it hard. Our ego is in fact hard. Hence, take small steps to drop your ego. The ego wants his or her point of view to survive. Learn to do things that the ego does not want. Slowly break the adamant ego. Learn to be flexible, learn to pray and ask for divine help. It will arrive. God is waiting to serve us, but we have to make the request.

THE DIVINE KEY TO SPIRITUAL AWAKENING

The door of death is a great awakening to me.

One evening I was in a boat with some of my students. A sudden storm took us all by surprise and we were thrown off the boat. I was helping one of my students who did not know how to swim, to hold on to the boat. The rest were doing the same. In minutes, we found ourselves on the shore miraculously.

All of us experienced a great sense of aliveness. There was no fear at all. 'How did this happen?,' questioned everybody. The answer was simple and led to a great awakening in me. We did not have time for fear. We were all in pure action. There was no thinking about the past or the future. We were totally in the present. The magic of the present made us all alive.

To be present totally is a great experience.

Many indulge in dangerous sports to experience the thrill of the moment. In a dangerous sport, you are totally in the present. You cannot afford to think of the past or the future. The magic of the present is the secret of the thrill of surfing or hunting.

If one can be totally in the present, then one need not indulge in any dangerous sports to experience the magic of the present.

How does one always be in the present without going to the past or the future?

Be present, when you look back at the past; be present when you look at the future. Learn the art of being in the present. You will then be open and alive to the present. When you are in the present, you will find yourself without words. There is an unnecessary wording of the mind that goes on uninterruptedly and puts us either in the past or in the future. Our mind thus dominates and bullies our life. So be without words and you will be present in 'what is.' The moment your attention is focused on 'here and now,' a certain stillness opens up, which is life nourishing.

In yoga, there are seven centres, which represent the flowering of consciousness. The seventh centre represents the state of enlightenment.

Enlightenment is a state where one experiences oneself as beyond thought, where the mind is not dominating and one can be 'here and now.' If you observe your mind, you will find it chatters unnecessarily. It is constantly broadcasting something and you get identified with the broadcast - the thought. You fail to realize that you are a witness to the thought and not the thought itself. This witness is just a 'presence.' It is devoid of words. However, you get lost in the witnessed and miss the witnessing consciousness, which is the real you. This is meditation.

How should I practise meditation and bring enlightening consciousness as a living reality in my daily life?

Firstly, learn to be calm. Value calmness. Do not assume that being worried is natural and get trapped in that myth.

Secondly, the moment you are a witnessing consciousness, unnecessary thoughts will reduce. Learn not to language an experience but be without words. Use words only when needed, otherwise be devoid of them.

Thirdly, you will find your thoughts will further reduce. Learn not to identify with your inner self-talk. When thoughts come do not identify or participate in them. Do not say I like this or dislike that, as this is another form of identification.

You will slowly slip into a witnessing consciousness and thus a new 'presence' opens up within you. Whenever you are free, for example, while in flight, observe your breath. The breath is in the present, and thus by observing your breath you will also be in the present. If you are driving, do not observe your breath, but be alive to the present. Be open to it without verbalising it. Practise the art of being in the present and see the miracle happening in your consciousness.

How does prayer help enlightenment?

More than prayer, it is prayerfulness that helps. Just be prepared and available for the divine. You cannot go after the Lord, for you do not know his address. Nevertheless, the Lord knows your address. You should be worthy for His grace to descend. Then you will find yourself enlightened.

Reflect on these stories.

A fragile built Zen master used to push huge rocks. When someone sought the secret of his strength, he said, 'I pray to the rocks and the rocks also help me mysteriously. Suddenly some force makes it all happen.'

A Chinese carpenter used to make masterpiece furniture. When asked how he could make them consistently, he replied that he would go to the trees and prayerfully make a request to fell them. Only when a tree would give him an intuitive nod, he would cut that tree. Thus each piece of furniture was a masterpiece. Let your prayer teach you how to surrender, prepare and be patient.

We are unhappy because we have chosen to be so. Why then, does one choose to be unhappy?

There is no other reason except ignorance. If unhappiness exists, we keep it alive; we identify ourselves with it. We say, it will take time for the unhappiness to vanish, but because we give time, we keep unhappiness alive.

Learn to surrender unhappiness and believe that the impossible will happen. If it does not, then there is a cosmic purpose. Allow it to be. If you can surrender your ego that life should happen the way you define, then a spiritual energy will descend. Ego brings with it an ordinary energy, whereas surrender brings a spiritual or a divine energy.

By surrender, you transcend the physical body and enter the spiritual body. In the environment of a spiritual body, you experience what is beyond the known structure of logic.

How will this understanding of surrender help us in our work and family lives?

In relationships, the greatest conflict is the expression of ego. Ego wants to prove a point. More than happiness, people want their point of view to survive. Thus, when their point of view is not fulfilled, they are unhappy and they nurture this unhappiness from their ego.

If one can surrender the ego and allow the cosmic plan to guide them, the surrendering attitude will make them calm. One will learn to say yes to the river of life. In this space, something, beyond ego, will descend,... the spiritual energy.

In this spiritual energy, one will be in touch with the spiritual body. This spiritual body will make one's relationship divine. One will experience a sense of sacredness and not sensuousness. Even in a sexual act, if one has gone beyond the mind, one experiences oneself beyond the body. One will come in touch with the spiritual energy. By surrendering, one will leap from the ordinary consciousness to a spiritual consciousness.

Most quarrels between men and women are due to their minds vomiting at each other. Their minds dominate them. By surrender, one is in the present. This 'presence,' and not the noisy mind, will touch the other in a silent way. A noisy mind leaks energy thereby sapping and depleting the other's energy. In a surrendered state, one's 'presence' will nourish the other.

In a relationship, one has to either say yes or no. However, a yes or no coming from the ego is reactive and filled with negativity that will infect the other. Remember that a thought can be conveyed as an infection or affection.

If 'yes' or 'no' comes from the spiritual body with an attitude of surrender, then it is pro-active; filled with positive energy that nourishes the other. By nourishing each other, each one grows into a beautiful being in a relationship.

Will this surrendering attitude help in business and the corporate world?

When you are egoistic, you will be caught in a rat race. In this rat race, even if you win, you will continue to be a rat.

You can do business effectively, without ego. You are not trying to prove yourself. From a spiritual body, you will work for excellence. You will see that excellence is the expression of the divine. If your competitor is better than you are, then you will learn from him. God in his divine ways will be guiding you. A spiritual body born out of purity is interested in learning, being in harmony and committed to excellence. This spiritual body emerges only when one surrenders one's ego. Surrender is not just renouncing, but accepting something nobler to fill your being.

SELF OBSERVATION
THE ART OF BEING WISE

The object of spiritual awakening is to make people think for themselves by the material called life. Life is the field of experience. The teaching is to make us think in a way that awakens us. Ordinary life makes us go into deep sleep. Since we have been living in the basement of our life, we miss the joy of exploring its higher dimensions. As you think differently, you will find yourself awake to deeper realities. You will realize that you are not just the body and the mind but also beyond them. Then you will come in touch with your spiritual body.

When people claim that their life is happy or unhappy, a question arises as to whether it is the result of an external situation or their internal moods. A person may be in the best of external situations, but internally unpleasant and thus his experience of the external will be a reflection of his internal world.

How many of us really take care of the internal world?

Most of us are lost in making the external beautiful. Observe when people talk about their life history. Generally it revolves around the events of the external situation that impacted or influenced their life. However, apart from events, there are 'states of being.' Our life does not solely depend on events but also depends on our states of being.

Can you give an example to convey the distinction between the inner states and the external events?

I have a young driver and an old maid servant. The old maid servant has been serving me for many years. I live in the Silicon Valley of India, the City of Bangalore. I have a beautiful garden and my residence is like a little heaven. Both of them quarrel frequently to prove that each one is more close to me than the other. They live in an external situation, which is like heaven, but internally they are experiencing hell. Their inner states truly determine the real quality of life.

How will this understanding of events and the inner states help me in my family life?

The quality of your relationship depends on your inner development. Relationships generally thrive on the lie that if the outer is fine then our life will also be fine. However, if one is aware that the quality of life depends on one's inner states, then the apparatus for living ….. the inner states have to be kept pure and alive.

If there is a difference or quarrel, one will work on one's inner states and not blame the other.

Suppose, you find that your husband is very sad and loves being sad, then you will know that he will not be happy by changing the external events. You have to work on his inner states. This clarity gives you great strength and direction.

How do we keep our internal state always positive so that the external events do not affect us? Can you elaborate through an inspiring example?

A teacher took a small glass and asked her students, 'How heavy is this glass?'

She got several answers. However, one kid got up and said, 'Madam, It all depends. If you hold the glass for one minute there is one unit of weight. If you hold it for one hour, it will weigh more and if you hold it for one day, it would torture you.'

Responses are relative. If you hold the glass for a minute, then keep it down, again pick it up after a while and continue the process, then holding the glass any number of times, does not matter.

Similarly, if some one insults you, you experience a little amount of hurt and if you mentally hold it for days together, then the same unit of hurt or sorrow would torture you badly. Learn to leave or let go of your hurt from time to time. Do not hold it mentally for long. As a result, you will be able to manage your inner states wisely.

Do you mean to say that by managing the inner states we will be more effective in dealing with the external events? Will this insight help in corporate life too?

Yes, it is true. A business involves many events. More than the events, how you react to the events will determine the quality of your life. Your reactions to the events depend on your inner states. Therefore, let this be an exercise in living, an exercise in observation of events and how you are reacting or responding to the events which depends on your inner states. Therefore, the external events become openings to reveal your inner states. Change the inner states and then you will be calm and more powerful. You will not become a victim of situations in life.

By observing, I go on changing myself and I find my mother-in-law does not change, is it not frustrating?

The external reality is that your mother-in-law is not changing. Your inner state is that you are reacting to it and hence you are feeling frustrated. Learn to be compassionate towards your mother-in-law. If your inner state is compassion, then love flows. You will be grateful to God that you are not as unwise as your mother-in-law is. You will learn from her, **not** to be like her. All this will happen if your inner state, your inner apparatus is pure.

If my mother-in–law takes me for granted, what should I do?

That is her problem. That is her weakness. Let your strength permit you not to be a victim of her weakness. That depends on your inner state and not on the external event. Learn to practise being an empty space like a flute. Out of emptiness, you make her realise your difficulties... thus make her aware as to how she is creating hell around her.

From that empty space if one expresses, then one is presenting one's point of view and not thrusting one's point of view.

How do I develop this inner purity?

Do not allow an impure mind to dominate you. Do not allow bad moods to dominate you. When bad moods occur, be a witness. Do not identify with them. See them like passing clouds. You are like space and thoughts are like clouds. Just learn the art of dis-identifying from your mind.

Can you elaborate on being pure?

The way you respond or react to the external events, show your state of being. Learn to be passive ..... do not react. To be passive requires your commitment to avoid mechanical reactions. Whenever you dis-identify, there is a passiveness that will diffuse reaction. The art of dis-identifying is an important spiritual discipline.

Can self-observation lead us to unity? I find myself pulled and pushed from none other than myself. What clarity do I need?

If you carefully observe you will realize that, you are not an individual but a crowd. There are multiple 'I's in us. There is a father, a son and a husband in you. These I's have different directions and pulls. If they do not have a common purpose, they become a crowd and not a unity.

How do I have a common purpose in the multiple I's as the roles are different?

The role of a husband, a father, a son, a boss ….. may be different. However, the common goal should be transformation, purity and goodness. If this is the common purpose, there is a unifying force that unites all the roles we play. Only then, do we become individuals or else we remain a crowd. Understand this clearly.

FLOAT AND NOT FIGHT IN THE OCEAN OF LIFE

Enjoy this moment and do not waste time brooding over the bad yesterday. Tomorrow may be even worse. One should learn to enjoy little things, for they exist in abundance.

Along with a few students of mine I had gone for a holiday in Hawaii after a hectic tour of North America. I was enjoying the beautiful beach in Hawaii. My brother's friend taught me how to float in the ocean. It was a great experience. In spite of being in the midst of huge waves I relaxed and floated along with them. Prior to learning to float, I used to be hit strongly by the waves. The moment I learnt to float, I was able to easily dance along with the waves.

Dead bodies do not drown but only people who are alive drown. That is because they fight with the ocean. In life, we should learn to float and not fight. This was a great learning experience.

How is it possible to float with life and not fight it? Isn't fight and struggle a part and parcel of life?

Please get the spirit of what is being said. Fight is also part of life. However, the art of wise living involves how one can be relaxed in life.

In martial arts like judo .... we observe how humble and relaxed the fighters are. Learn to relax. Even if you have to fight, be alert and relaxed. For example, if you encounter a snake and are tense, you may fall on the snake and harm yourself. Alternatively, if you are alert and relaxed, you may not have to kill the snake; it may just pass away.

Fight when required; your fight will then be from a flow of relaxation.

When my boss or my mother-in-law shout at me how can I be relaxed and float in the moment?

Whilst learning to float in the ocean, I asked myself the same question. When a powerful wave approaches shouldn't I be running away from it? However, after having learnt to float, even when a powerful wave came I was able to float very easily along with the wave.

Similarly, when your boss is shouting at you, just keep your body relaxed and be alert to what he is saying. When you are alert, your mind is calm. Your body is a good anchor to play with. Just relax any tense portion in your body. The intention to relax, will make the body relax. Remember that a tensed body creates a tensed mind and a tense mind impacts the body again. Make relaxation a part of life even when you eat, take a bath, walk... Let all your movements have a quality of relaxation.

How is it possible for me to relax my body at the time when someone is talking harshly to me?

It is possible. Intend strongly that relaxation should happen and it will. All creativity has happened by the power of intention. The possibility of anything happening is possible only when you see it as a possibility in your mind. When you are learning a new language it appears impossible, but with a strong commitment, it becomes possible. In my workshops, I make people sit in uncomfortable positions, instructing them to further worsen their sitting stance little by little. Finally, I tell them to sit down in a comfortable position and further make themselves more comfortable. By doing this process, I make people realize then one can further anything by using their power of intention.

Is only learning to relax the body and mind sufficient or is something else also required?

Learn to relax your emotions too. This can be achieved if you can diffuse anger as it emerges. Learn to superimpose a happy emotion over it. Think of a happy moment. Do not allow the anger to pile up. Learn to see the object of anger in a humorous way.

Apply the superimposing technique and change the emotion. While doing that, keep the body, not only relaxed, but also alive. Keep it enthusiastic. The energy of the body will impact your emotions also.

But is all this not manipulation?

So what if it is manipulation. You are changing yourself to a better state. When you are sick, are you not administered medicines? Are you not told to move your body, even if you do not want to do? You can call this by any word. The true intention is to uplift yourself, so that you can be in a better state. What is wrong in doing that? Also when you get negative emotion, see what it wants, what it is trying to say, which wound it is trying to protect. Use your intellect and understand your negative emotions.

What do you mean when you say, 'negative emotions are trying to convey something?'

A female student called me on my mobile. It was a long distance call. She said, she had a bad headache and her examination was to start in two days. She could not study and she was worried. I told her to find out what her headache was trying to convey. I made her talk to her headache and she said, it wanted her to freak out that day. I told her to do that. She cried, 'What about my examination?' I told her to freak out as she could not study with a headache. Within three hours, she gave me a call saying that her headache had vanished. Then I advised her to study.

Learn to talk to your negative emotions and discover their hidden agenda. They communicate through the language of pain.

Why can't I be honest when I get angry, I just get angry and be authentic to my negative emotions? Why play games and change the negative into a positive?

Continue this logic and you will end up in hell. If you feel like killing someone, will you be honest and kill him? I don't suppose so. When you are upset, be honest and say yes, I am upset. Then, will this upset help you? Since it will not help you, you should change. Dishonesty is when you are upset, you pose you are not and then justify that you are not upset or protect your being upset.

In this context, can you give us an inspiring story?

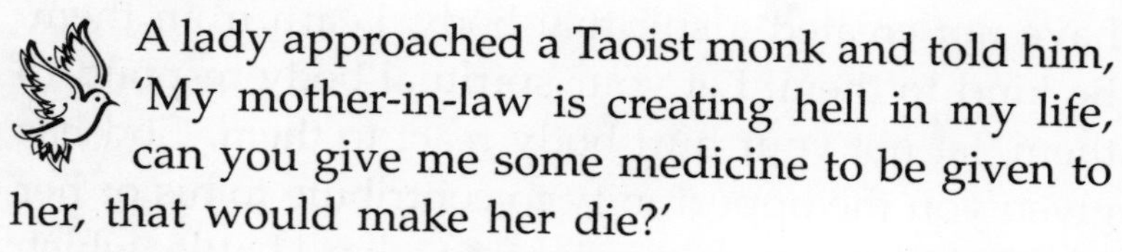

A lady approached a Taoist monk and told him, 'My mother-in-law is creating hell in my life, can you give me some medicine to be given to her, that would make her die?'

The monk gave her some medicine and asked her to mix it in tea before giving it to her mother-in-law. The only condition, he said, 'Be very kind and loving to her, only then would the medicine work. Also when she dies no one will suspect you. She will die after two months.'

After one month she returned to the monk and pleaded, 'I do not want my mother-in-law to die, she has changed. She is very kind to me nowadays.' The monk said, 'More than the medicine, it is your love that worked.'

Just bring your loving energy in whatever you do. See the miracle of love. It will uplift you and others too. In the power of love is God. God is not an entity, God is a principle. The principle of pure goodness.

I have seen that many people do not change in spite of giving them love and respect. Why is it so?

Let not love be barter. Do not treat love as a means to an end. Be loving and see you will be creating heaven in you. If some one does not change, understand every soul has a journey. Sometimes their journey has to be fulfilled.

Also understand, when some one does not change, it is because his or her hurt body is very strong. They have not created a spiritual body. Learn from them. Be kind to them. Let your spiritual body respond to them, let not your hurt body react to them. God has given you the opportunity to contribute to his or her life. Be kind, each one is fighting a hard battle, which one does not know.

So you are telling us, to keep the body relaxed and vibrant, to keep one's emotion pure, mind calm and understanding. Is there anything more?

There is much more. Do not take all this knowledge and decorate your intellect. Then it will be like a donkey carrying sandalwood. You have to practise it. When you practise then your being will be sacred. At present, we have a sensuous mind, not a sacred mind. Once your being is sacred a spiritual apparatus would be created. Then intelligence would flow. Knowledge does not really bless us; it is intelligence that uplifts us.

How will this understanding help me in my business life?

In many ways, it will help you. In a tense situation, if you keep your body relaxed, then it is good to your body. When you are relaxed, healthy chemicals will be released. When you are tense, unhealthy chemicals will be produced, which is not good for you.

When your body is relaxed and vibrant you will be in a better state. So keeping your mind calm and learning, new possibilities will open up. Walt Disney looked at a rat and got his idea of Mickey Mouse. Keeping your emotions in a positive mood, will make you powerful. In many ways, what I have taught you will help in business and corporate life.

If you do not practise this, you will be in an unresourceful state, which will overpower you and not empower you.

We make our lives

Man is his life. Our lives are series of experiences. As is the experience, so is life. If a person's experiences are unhappy, his life is unhappy and vice versa. A single day in one's life is a small replica of one's whole life. If man is unable to work towards change for even a day in his life, then he will not be able to change his life. To change his life, he has to change every moment.. every day. If he does not change but says he is working on changing himself, then it is just a figment of his imagination.

To change one's life, one has to observe. Observe one's body, mind, feelings, values, and observe as to how one responds to the various situations in life. But if one gives excuses of changing from tomorrow, then one will never work on changing today, but only postpone it to tomorrow. This is one of the gravest diseases in spirituality.

In order to truly work on changing oneself, one has to define one's work. The field of one's work is today.

How do I know that I am working on the process of changing myself?

The true quality of work is to observe your reactions to the situations in life. Are you reacting or responding to situations? If you are reacting to a situation, then the situation is controlling you, but if you are responding to it then your commitment is guiding you. For instance, when someone scolds you and you react, then the situation is controlling you but if you pause and observe your behaviour or question whether you should remain quiet or ignore him or answer him back .... then you are bringing your 'presence,' your conscious 'presence' to the situation. This is a response. The true responsibility is the ability to respond.

I see my reactions as being mechanical. I feel I am a machine, a robot. What do I do?

You are conscious of the fact that your reactions are mechanical. The very fact that you are conscious shows that you are not a machine but a conscious being. Draw your energy from this consciousness. At present, you are not anchored in the 'presence' of your consciousness. Your 'I' is in the 'mechanicalness.' Your 'I' should be anchored in your consciousness. Bring this 'presence' in your daily activities of life.

What should my action plan be in my daily activities of life?

Bring the 'presence' of consciousness in your daily activities. The spiritual work-exercise is to bring consciousness in small activities of life. Be conscious of your reactions and be aware if your feelings have purity or the garbage of negativity. Be conscious of your voice. Is your body relaxed or tense? Are your thoughts compulsive? Can you be inwardly empty, free from the unnecessary thoughts? Observe your self-talk. Find out whether your self-talk guides or distracts you.

Why is my mind always talking? Is this self-talk essential or unessential?

Our minds are constantly dominating our lives. We are entrapped by our minds and they become our enemies. Mind has a self-talk mechanism. Having compulsive thoughts is a psychological disorder.

As we have not raised the level of our consciousness, our mind keeps on chattering.

Do this exercise; just as a tiger waits and watches out for its prey, wait and watch out for thoughts that arise. At this moment shut your eyes, and observe the first, second and the third thought in that order. Do it right now.

You will observe that no thoughts arise. When you are alert, thoughts do not arise. In the space of alertness, your 'presence' is more conscious. When your 'presence' has less consciousness, there are more thoughts.

Hence when the mind is constantly talking, it indicates that your level of consciousness has not increased. More thoughts are a symptom of being less conscious.

Consciously use your self-talk when required and when not required learn to be inwardly empty.

How do I eliminate negative thoughts in my mind?

Understand that every thought creates a subtle substance. Negative thought creates a hurt body; positive thought creates a bliss body. The bliss body will uplift you while the hurt body will make you a victim of circumstances in life.

Secondly, whenever a negative thought arises, learn to dis-identify from it. See yourself as a witness and the thought as witnessed by you. You are the subject and the thought is an object. You are an observer and the thought is the observed. Slowly distance yourself from the thought.

Thirdly, observe how dominating your mind is and how compulsive thoughts are being processed.

Finally, as far as possible, let there be absence of words. Learn to develop the taste of being without any self-talk.

What spiritual benefit does one achieve when negative thoughts are eliminated?

Purification happens. In this purification, our centres become receptive to allow the higher vibrations to flow in. New ideas become understandable. If our centres are not purified, divine messages, new ideas… will not flow in. We should thus insulate ourselves from negativity and keep our centres pure and receptive, so that the higher states of consciousness can guide us.

Will this purity help us in our corporate life as well?

As said previously, our centres when purified are available for higher vibrations. Creativity happens in this space. The great Indian musician Thyagaraja, listening to a bee discovered a new raga... a musical note. A monk observing a snake and a crane fighting discovered the martial art called Tai Chi.

Would you please elaborate on creativity?

There is a technique called the golden egg technique…. imagine, there is an egg and in it there exists gold. This gold is hidden in the egg. In a similar manner, treat every problem as such an egg and realise that there is gold or opportunity hidden inside. Whenever you are faced with a problem, do not get disheartened but understand that it is only an egg having gold hidden in it. Delve deep into the problem and see the gold of opportunities. This attitude will invoke creativity in you.

Is there any other technique on creativity?

There are many more. Whenever there is a problem, think of twenty ways of solving it. Like a game, write down twenty ways of solving a problem. Choose five ways out of the twenty and work on them. With those five ways find twenty ways of fulfilling them. Ask your friends to give ideas. The mother of creativity is generating ideas. Play with it.

Can I use this method in motivating my lazy son?

All these methods can be applied provided you remember not to view a problem as a pain. If you do so, then your hurt body will increase and you will pass on your pain to your son. Instead, apply the golden egg technique. In the problem of your lazy son, there is gold hidden... an opportunity hidden. Treat it as a great opportunity to study the reason as to why he is lazy. Be an anthropologist and study the causes of his laziness. By doing this you are in a pro-active state and this state of your being will motivate your son.

Next, apply the second method. See twenty ways to make your son active. Take help from friends .... thereby expanding your ideas. Creativity opens up when there are ideas. Include your son in the game plan and make him your team-mate. You will observe the inspiring energy that you create and as a result your family will have a meaningful goal.

Can I adopt this technique with my nagging wife?

First and foremost stop conveying to your wife that she is a nag. Use transformational vocabulary .... use empowering language. The moment you tell her she is a nagging wife, she will retort immediately accusing you, which would result in a war of words. This will affect the flower of your love. Once you start using words, you bring in logic leading to arguments. There are no winners in an argument. Hence use words wisely. When your wife expresses something, try and understand her point of view instead of branding and labelling her. The moment you brand her, you will be blinded and will see only the labels. As a result you miss seeing the real person.

How can we become richer by differences in a relationship?

Stop treating differences as conflicts. View them as points of view. Learn to appreciate variety. Appreciate differences rather than viewing them as pain. The moment you relate to differences as pain, you will experience them as pain. View differences as other ways of looking at a situation.

Absence of words

It was a beautiful evening. Clouds hovered like celestial beings. As one looked out of the window, one could see the trees green with celestial lustre and flowers dancing with joy. The perceiver is filled with wonder at this wonderful happening. How is it that some experience wonder while others do not? Is it not because of sensitivity? The grass filled with life... their size, the space and the magical world is beyond the description of words. Yet, why do we depend on words? Why have words become so important? Why do we invest in them?

> ***I find the presence of my husband irritating? I love him and at the same time dislike him? Why this contradiction?***

Observe how your mind is constantly dominating and manipulating your life. You need to put an end to its domination. You can do that if you understand that mind is nothing but words. Learn to be in the absence of words. When a person is verbose inwardly, his 'presence' is heavy. If you sit under a tree, you feel its 'presence' to be nourishing. Similarly, if you sit next to a silent man you will bathe in his serenity.

Your verbose mind conveys to you that your husband is irritating. See your husband without the seer. Perceive him without the perceiver. The perceiver is burdened with memory, with words, with dogmas and hence is not sensitive to 'what is.' We do not see a person 'as he is,' but 'as he should be.'

The fact has to be seen. The seeing is not through words or your likes and dislikes. Zen meditation involves being in the 'presence' of the river and seeing it without words. A deep sacredness arises with such quality of seeing.

Therefore, see your husband in the absence of any words and experience sacredness.

But why do I love and hate him? Why can't I be consistent in my love?

Mind spins its own logic. We are victims of our own logic. We have rules, which decide when the flower of love should be and when it should not be. Our love is born out of thoughts. A love born out of thoughts is destroyed by a thought. Thoughts are sitting on the throne of our life. We are imprisoned by thoughts. Can we free our love from the prison of thoughts? Our dislike is also born out of a thought. Thoughts change and hence love and dislike change accordingly.

Is there something more to a conflict of relationship?

Everyone has rules, which tell us, if this happens I will love him and if it does not happen I will hate him. These rules control our lives. We rarely inspect the sanity of these rules, which dictate our lives. Our lives are imprisoned by them. We have to see how these rules confine us, even though it is an illusion. In fact we are like the space, which cannot be confined. Can the room confine space? Space exists in the room. But it appears that the room limits the space, for we look at space from the angle of the room. But the fact remains that the room exists in space and does not limit it.

Similarly, it appears that we are limited by rules. This is an illusion. But the illusion will act as reality as long we don't see it as an illusion.

Can you see that the 'I' is free from the rules? If you operate from this 'I' and not the 'I' confined by the rules, then this is salvation or *Moksha*.

How can I perceive without the perceiver? I am the perceiver; hence the limitation of the perceiver exists and should exist. Please clarify.

If we try to understand truth from the confinement of our known structure of logic, then we will end up like a frog in the well, which assumed that the well was the world.

Reflect on this story.

A little fish went around seeking the ocean in the ocean itself. It went around asking other fishes as to where the ocean was. 'This is the ocean,' replied other fishes. But the little fish was not convinced. An elderly fish, guided the little fish to the shore, and pushed it out of the ocean. The little fish started gasping for life. The elderly fish helped the little fish back into the ocean. 'Why did you do that,' screamed the little fish.

'This itself is the ocean,' replied the elderly fish.

Stop seeking like the little fish. There is nothing you have to seek in order to see something. What you have to do is to just 'look.'

Yes. You are the perceiver. But can you perceive without the limitations of the perceiver? The limitations of the perceiver are his boundary of knowledge and memory. The perceiver for reference has his knowledge, ignorance and memory. The 'I' exists beyond the limitation of knowledge, ignorance and memory. One can use knowledge and memory, but not get limited by it. One can use it as a reference, but not as an identity. When we perceive without the perceiver, we do not see from the thought, but from the pure being. In this space, a different type of looking emanates.

Have you seen some people look at others from their opinions, likes and dislikes? Are they really looking? Their opinion, likes and dislikes will start interfering in their perception. Hence, learn to free yourself from this trap and just look, purely from innocence.

Is it not right to have the limitations of the perceiver?

If that is your choice and decision, let it be so. If you accept limitation, then the limitation is yours, but if you accept limitlessness, then limitlessness is yours. Why does a person want more and more of everything..? The 'more' is ultimately seeking for limitlessness. Limitation is like dust in your eyes. As long as it exists, your effort is to eliminate it, because it is a foreign particle. In a similar manner limitation is a foreign particle. So your effort should be to eliminate it.

Understand, infinite is not other than finite. If infinite is other than finite, then infinite becomes finite, for it is other than finite. Infinite is in-spite of finite. It includes finite and is not limited by finite. In the same way, limitlessness includes limitation and is not other than limitation.

How does this understanding of perceiving without the perceiver help in a father and son relationship?

Very often a father gets stuck in his opinion of his son. In spite of his son changing, he cannot see it. His identity of himself and his son limits the quality of his perception. So also, the son is stuck in his opinion of his father and sees the sky through his own window ... thereby assuming, that the sky is limited to the shape of his window.

Reflect on this incident:

I was travelling to the airport with a student of mine in Milan, Italy. He had seen the ticket several times and felt that the flight was scheduled at 4.45 pm. The flight was to actually take off at 6.45 am. As a result, I missed the flight. While we were in San Francisco we were told that we had to reach Milan airport at 4.45 pm. He mistook 'am' as 'pm.' That thought got stuck in his mind and in spite of seeing the particulars on the ticket several times, he read it as 4.45 pm. In the same manner, we form an opinion and later start seeing others from that opinion. Hence, the perceiver limits the perception. Relationships will be liberating if we can practise this quality of seeing. Or else a father still sees his grown up son as a child.

I experience a sense of heaviness. Is this heaviness a result of the perceiver loaded with likes, dislikes, conclusions, dogmas.....?

True. There is a 'law of gravitation' and a 'law of grace.' In occultism, the law of gravitation is that which pulls us to the earth, our attachments, likes and dislikes .... when one is pure, one experiences a sense of lightness and also experiences the law of grace - a movement towards heaven. Heaven is not a place, but is a state of being where one experiences a sense of relaxation and lightness.

To rise to the level of the stars is the law of grace. This is opposed to the law of gravitation that drags us down to the earth. Why do you want to be limited to the earth, when you can fly up to the sky? Why be a dwarf when you can be a giant?

Why do you cling to your ignorance, your impurity that keeps you low? This makes you ugly. You can grow to the heights of purity, kindness, forgiveness and bliss. Allow that to happen by dropping your likes, dislikes, anger, jealousy....

What constitutes the soul of the law of grace is inner freedom. Free yourself from all limitations of the mind, its likes and dislikes.

Have you observed that whenever you are angry or sad, you feel very heavy and burdened? This is the law of gravitation. Have you also observed that whenever you are loving, kind, inwardly free, you feel you are floating and flying?

This is the law of grace.

Alignment of the Three Centers

When you face difficulties and contradictions, do not try to break them but mould them with love, kindness and humility. Give them time to heal. In that space a different energy will flow in your lives. There are two energies – one, an ordinary energy that supports ego, provides a reason for it to exist and gives deceptive goals; the other, a divine energy that dilutes and destroys the ego. This will make you look at life differently. For that energy to flow in, it is necessary that we prepare ourselves prayerfully, proceed positively and pursue persistently.

There are three centres in us that need to be aligned. It is like tuning a TV or a radio. These are... the body, emotions and intellect. When all three centres are aligned in your daily life, a divine energy flows and a magical transformation occurs. You will then find trees to be greener, the sun being radiant and stars magically shining conveying experiences without words.

How do you align the moving, the emotional and the intellectual centres? What are they?

The moving centre is the body. Body constantly moves .... your blood, your breath etc. The body centre has to be relaxed and happy. The important aspect in *yoga* is to relax the body. Whatever you are doing, learn to do it in a relaxed way - the way you sit, bathe..... keep it very relaxed. The very intention to relax will make it happen.

When you relax, healthy chemicals are generated in your body whereas in tension, unhealthy chemicals spread. So learn to relax.

Can you give a story to convey this point?

Four people were on a plane; a pilot, a politician, a teacher and a student. Mid-air, the pilot announced, 'Something is wrong with the aircraft. There are only 3 parachutes and I am an important person...' he took one parachute and jumped out.

The politician hearing this, hurriedly said, 'I am also very important person...' he took another and jumped out.

The teacher advised the student, 'I have lived my life. You take the last parachute and save yourself.'

The student said, 'Master, there are still two more parachutes and both of us can be saved.'

The teacher exclaimed, 'How can that be! Two have already jumped out. Hence, there must be only one parachute.'

The student answered, 'Master, the politician was in such a great hurry… he took my school bag and jumped.'

When you are in tension, there are more reasons for you to be ineffective. Learn to keep your body relaxed in whatever action you perform. Also, let your being be happy. How do you do that? Just try to be happy. Learn to smile more often. Practise laughing meditation …. just laugh without any reason. The best antidote for anger is laughter. When anger arises, go to a bathroom and laugh it out and you will find anger energy that gives tension, will slowly diffuse.

One can purify the body centre by being relaxed and happy.

What about the other two centres - the emotional and intellectual?

Just watch your emotions each moment. They can be negative or positive. Don't allow the negative emotion to rule your life. Whenever a negative emotion like jealousy arises, just dis-identify with it. View it from a distance. Let your 'I' not be in that emotion.

Learn to bring forth love and kindness in all your feelings. Let there be a flowing energy in you. Bring that energy in all your movements.

Is there any technique to bring out the positive emotions in my life?

As anchor, wear a chain or a ring or keep a precious stone. Once in a while, remember to use it as a trigger to generate positive emotions. All that you have to practise is to remember the anchor in order to generate the positive emotion. You can even chant the name of the Lord and bring out devotion.

Make a habit to bring out positive emotion in all walks of your daily life. By purifying your emotional centre, you will be open to divine vibrations.

How does one purify ones intellectual centre?

Always keep your mind calm and void. Keep the mind open and receptive, as every difficult situation teaches something profound. Be a good finder. If someone creates problems, observe what existence tries to teach you through them.

Can you give an example from your personal experience with respect to purifying intellect?

Once I had to tell one of my students, 'It is frustrating dealing with you.' But I said it lovingly. This resulted in surfacing her childish behaviour. Sometimes I use strong words to wake people up. She was very unhappy. I counselled her saying that my words were from love and not out of anger. My counselling lasted nearly 3 days. I asked myself what I learnt from this. I found that I had learnt something very profound. A person hears a word and then mentally adds personal 'overtones' to it. If a word has five units of tenor, her personal 'overtones' will add 90 units to it, thereby she experiences 95 units of sorrow.

All that I told her was that it was frustrating to deal with her. My tenor in the word frustrating was

5 units, whereas the person added 90 units. Hence the word frustrating generated great sorrow!

This one incident helped me in purifying my intellect to a great extent.

Supposing a father tells his son, 'You are stupid,' the son may mentally add a voice that can literally harm him by interpreting that his father does not love him.

The key expression is 'Watch yourself.'

Do we need to combine the body, the emotion and the intellect centres in all our daily activities?

By keeping one's body relaxed and being happy, one can bring in positive emotion. By keeping one's intellect open and calm, there is an alignment that happens. In every activity, ensure that all three centres are aligned. Thus, a transformational apparatus gets created. Divine energy will then start flowing in one's life. One will start looking at life differently. This is *yoga* ... meaning 'joining.' Join all the three centres in a purified way. Sacredness will emerge in your life.

When a neighbour says something very irritating what can one learn from it?

Be kind. Your neighbour is fighting a hard battle. May be God has given you the opportunity to be kind enough. See how your neighbour's mind is programmed to be in sorrow. See it as a result of one's programming.

Apply the technique of seeing yourself as a transparent being. Let harsh words pass through you. Do not be like a wall ... otherwise, harsh words will clash with you. Be an empty space and let harsh words pass through you. J. Krishnamurthy used to say, 'When a dog barks and you resist, there is a clash. But if you don't resist, it will pass through.'

Treat life as a training ground. Dealing with a difficult neighbour provides you with an opportunity to grow.

Can this help in being a good leader and thereby developing leadership skills?

When body, emotion and intellect are aligned and purified, there will be charisma in one's being. Such a being will be radiant for divine energy to flow in. One's 'presence' will be empowering and not overpowering. It is not through words that one can motivate others. It is by one's being, by one's 'presence.' It is said when a snake bit *Mahavira,* milk oozed and not blood. His being was as loving as that of a mother.

By aligning the three centres, a transformational apparatus would be created, resulting in a different level of knowing. A powerful leader should also learn from bad situations in life. One of the gurus of Dattatreya was a hen. Dattatreya saw a hen scraping garbage for a grain. Similarly in the garbage of difficulties, let us look for good things in life and not get lost in worries. In life, we may be in the midst of garbage, but if we look carefully, there are seeds of wisdom!

Inspiration
THE FATHER OF CREATIVITY

A farmer had an old donkey. One day, the donkey fell into a dry well. The farmer tried his best to rescue the donkey but failed. Finally he decided to let the old donkey die by burying it in the well itself.

He took a spade and started filling the well with debris. The donkey being a wise one, shook off the debris from its body as and when debris fell on it. This continued for a while. Suddenly, the farmer was surprised to find the donkey emerging from the well. The continuous shaking off the debris helped the donkey to come out of the well.

It gives a great insight. Shake it off and step up. People may throw garbage, but shake the garbage off and step up and life will be different and divine.

But why do people abuse and throw garbage on us? How can I be still inspired in spite of my boss and others throwing garbage at me?

'Garbage in' is 'garbage out.' One can give what one has. Once you understand this, you will be kind. You cannot expect a scorpion to kiss you. People around, with their hurt bodies create pain for others. Their minds are so noisy that they create noise. Be an anthropologist and study unhappy people. If Victor Franklin could do that why can't you do so? He was in a Nazi jail for ten years and studied how some people could bear the torture and some could not. After being released from jail, he wrote a beautiful book - Man in Search of Meaning. He said that one thing the Nazis could not do to him was to take away his attitude. Remember, the success of most people depends on 90% attitude and 10% situation. Many studies validate this.

Be like the donkey in the story, shake it off and step up.

Quite often, we hold on to what has happened in our lives. We mentally hold on to the pain for a week, a month and create a hurt body in us. We cannot shake it loose from our memory. The hurt body starts eating our joy. It starts re-living the experience of abuse and creates a mountain out of a molehill. Observe and try to change. We have a choice to keep an abuse within us or live or re-live with it or shake it off.

Why do we suffer in pain and recreate it moment to moment?

As I told you, thought creates energy. If thought is negative, then energy is negative. The negative energy creates pain. A hurt body looks at the world through pain. A hurt body will try its best to sustain pain. It is a matter of survival. So, it loves to attract pain and sustain pain. It will use logic to protect it. Look at unhappy people. They will convince you to be miserable.

How do we get out of the hurt body? What is a way out?

All that you can do is to create a bliss body in you. There are 5 layers in you.

- Physical body
- Pranic body… breath body.
- Mental body
- Intellectual body
- Bliss body

All these layers in us have energies. It is in potential form. Just as there is latent fire in wood and by rubbing the wood it is invoked. In the same way you have to awaken the physical body through exercise, yoga, dance, balanced diet…. Keep the body alive and enthusiastic. You will then awaken a happy energy through the body.

The *pranic* or breath body has to be awakened. Breathe deeply by *pranayama* and find a different kind of joy surfacing in you. Shallow breathing creates lower energy field while deep breathing enhances one's aliveness.

Mental body can be awakened, if you keep your mind calm. A calm mind has a different joy; a noisy mind is an avenue for leakage of energy.

When your intellect is open and receptive, yet another dimension of blissful energy arises. One who is open and receptive is always learning. Children learn very fast as their intellect is open and receptive.

Bliss body in oneself has to be opened up. In deep sleep, bliss body opens up naturally. In waking state, if one is committed to be happy and learn to look at life in a celebrative way, a bliss centre will be awakened.

When these five layers are opened, as the *Vedas* - the Hindu scriptures say, a bliss body is created. This is the way to heaven.

Opening five bodies or layers - is it a form of prayer?

Yes. Prayer is not changing God. Prayer is changing oneself. A lot of people feel by praying, we remind God as to what he has to do to us. In a temple, one rings a bell. It is not to wake God, but to awaken the God within. God exists within, but the five layers that have not opened are like closed doors. Prayer is to open these inner layers of ourselves.

Will my nagging husband change, if he opens the five layers within? How will our relationship improve by applying these insights?

If we are depleted, there is leakage of energy. We then try to draw energy from our partner. Each one starts sapping the other's energy. Thus we become dependent on the other. The other feels miserable if one is dependent and saps one's energy. Then one becomes possessive. No one likes to be possessed. Freedom is our birthright. We feel bound if some one possesses us. This leads to pushing the partner out of the freedom zone. The partner feels rejected. This rejected self will maintain a mental score and will wait to settle scores in the times to come. By this, a war of roses will occur.

But if you have tapped all the five layers within you, you will overflow with joy. Share joy but not beg for it. You will not sap the energy of the other as you are already overflowing. You will neither be dependent on the other nor be independent. But if you learn to be interdependent, your partner will feel a sense of belonging. The relationship will reach new heights when you open your body, *prana*, mind, intellect and bliss centres.

What are the signs of an enlightened relationship?

One has to get out of addictive demands in a relationship. Husband and wife are usually lost in their demands and thus miss the 'here and now.' Being present 'here and now' creates a different 'presence.' A spouse whether alone or with the partner should know how to be present 'here and now.' We are generally lost either in the past or in the future but not alive to the present.

The relationship between a husband and a wife should not be based on demands but one can have preferences. Understand the distinction between demand and preference. Demand makes one rigid and overpowering... meaning without, *this*, 'I' refuse to be happy, while preference makes one light and inclusive... means 'I' prefer *this*, but if it does not happen it is OK. It makes one more flexible.

Another sign of an enlightened relationship is an understanding that happiness is within. A partner is one who helps you to go within. 'The kingdom of heaven is within you,' quotes the Bible. 'Happiness is within us,' declares the Gita.

Is it OK to be selfish in a relationship?

Yes. Start with selfishness, but move towards a unified self. Do not invest in selfishness, as this will lead to compulsiveness. There is nothing wrong in catering to oneself. But have the vision of yourself being inclusive and not exclusive. Love is inclusive whereas likes are exclusive. Let your relationship be based on love and not on 'likes.'

How can I see the foolishness of selfishness?

The earth is small speck of dust in this cosmos. Two thirds of the earth is covered with water. The remaining one thirds includes forests, mountains, landmass ….. The country you live is insignificant in the cosmos. In this, there are many species and you are just one amongst them. Where are you in this macrocosm? You are very tiny and insignificant but you live as though you are the most important person in this cosmos. Can you see your foolishness?

How [illegible] face the foolishness [illegible] selfishness?

The earth [illegible] a speck of [illegible] two thirds of the earth is covered [illegible]. The remaining [illegible] includes [illegible] mountains, lands [illegible] inhabited [illegible] live [illegible] of the cosmos [illegible], there are many [illegible] and you are just one [illegible] them. [illegible] this [illegible] [illegible] very [illegible] important but [illegible] the most important person [illegible]. Can you see your [illegible]?

Witness

THE INNER FLOWERING

Lord Buddha was once meditating. His mind started creating problems and distracted him from the path of enlightenment. His state of mind was like that of hundreds of horses galloping at a time. But Buddha just remained a witness and did not identify with fear. His mind turned into thousands of elephants tempting him to identify with them, but Buddha was just a witness ... he saw through the game of his mind. His mind became a loving deer but still Buddha reminded a witness. His mind tried all its ways to tempt him but Buddha remained a witness.

Finally, his mind turned into a loving child drowning in the ocean, seeking his attention. Buddha, out of compassion, merged with his thoughts and stretched out his hands to save the drowning child. At once, the child turned into a monster and started pulling Buddha to the ocean. Buddha realised his folly and left the monster and continued being a witness. The monster turned again into a child and started pleading for help.

Buddha continued his meditation of being not participating but by just being a witness. The child drowned in the ocean and emerged as an enlightened mind ...depicting Buddha's mind. This is a play narrating Buddha's effort towards enlightenment.

Similarly, our mind plays various games, but our commitment should be to watch and be a witness.

Is dis-identification an important aspect of meditation? What is worry?

Learn to be a witness to your thoughts and feelings. In the witnessing consciousness, there is no identification with anything. Identification leads to misery. Worry is a form of identification. Literally, worry means twisting and tearing. Have you observed that when you worry, your moving centre gets twisted? Negative state of worry – depression or fear ... shows up strongly in the form twisting of one's body - moving centre.

Just be a witness and do not get identified. Relax your body, your mind and then finally just be a witness. Let not your 'I' get identified with your body and mind. This dis-identification is meditation.

What about emotions in a state of worry?

Firstly, negative emotional states like habitual worrying, being jealous...must be seen and noticed. Generally we do not see them instead we become them. While a negative emotion is happening, just be an onlooker. Then the emotion will be like a cloud that comes and goes.

Through the intellectual centre create a new will, to stop a negative emotion that comes out. This is not suppression as you are doing it with an understanding that if negative emotion is let loose, it will create a hurt body. In turn this hurt body will take control of you.

Through the moving centre i.e your body - keep it relaxed and happy. The important issue here is being a witness and not getting identified.

Worry is a form of identification. It is useless. Unfortunately many of us think it is right to worry about some one we love. This is madness in motion. Give up this voluntary form of suffering.

By worrying you exhaust yourself and your energy gets depleted. In a depleted state, one cannot perform to the optimum level. Learn to take small steps, stop worrying, and do not give worry a ground to operate. Weed out the worry as it emerges. Do not allow the other centres to support and nourish it.

What do you mean when you say we live in two worlds?

One is visible and outer while the other is invisible and inner. The outer is your body that is visible. The inner is your psychology. The object of spiritual teaching is to lead a person from unconscious being to a conscious being.

Man realises that his body changes, but he does not realise that his mind also changes. He may agree that his body is in a wrong state but he refuses to accept that his mind also can be in a negative state.

In fact there is a third world, which is beyond one's body and mind. It is beyond time and space. It is the soul... the *atma*.

Can you dwell a little more on the inner world, the mind?

Generally, we are present physically in a place while being psychologically elsewhere. Outer seeing makes you see physically where you are. Inner seeing makes you see psychologically where you are. Just as how we visit different places physically so too, psychologically we wander through. Can we be alert to where we visit inwardly? Just as when we visit some place, if it is an unhealthy place, we fall sick or if it is a dangerous place, we may be endangered. Similarly, if we are in an unhealthy place inwardly, we fall sick. If one is in a dark room, one cannot see things clearly, but with the help of light one can see. By observing oneself, one can come to light and see oneself clearly. One will be in a state of joy - a healthy place and not in a state of worry - an unhappy place. This seeing is very important.

Is not observing oneself, seeing one's inner world a boring and a tedious work?

That it is boring is a movement of thought. If a thought verbalises it as boring, then it becomes boring.

Observe how we whip ourselves through self-talk. Why do you frequent yourself to negative self-talk? Observe and see how your hurt body wants to sustain this misery. Observing oneself is like driving a car - practical intelligence in motion.

Just as driving a car is useful to reach a destination, so also observing oneself is also important for reaching newer heights of joy.

Also when one observes oneself, one will come in touch with the world beyond thoughts. Real joy exists beyond one's mind.

But why should I observe myself, I am OK?

By observing yourself, you realise how your psychology is involved in the experience of a situation. If the psychology of your thinking is not pure then a situation is seen in a polluted way - not the external pollution, but the pollution of your mind.

Reflect on this conversation.

You say, 'I don't like Mr. John.'

'Can you see how your dislike is mechanical and programmed?'

'No. He is unfair and hence I dislike him.'

'You are also unfair.'

'No I am fair.'

'Can you see how mechanical you are in seeing yourself as fair?'

If we observe, the concept of fair and unfair is a product of your definition of fair and unfair. In a certain culture, having a relationship before marriage is fair and an expression of freedom. But in other cultures, it is a blemish or licentiousness. So often, our opinions are a product of social conditioning. Only through understanding, we set ourselves free from personal and social madness.

I know I am unfair and I justify it. Why is this so?

Any justification is a part of the struggle of a hurt body to survive. Some are aware of their justifying while others are not. One of the important teachings of great masters like Gurdjieff is, 'We are lying but we are not aware of our lying.' The first step is to realise our lying as one of the greatest blocks in the path of transformation. We lie and then justify it. If the state of our being is low... operating from lower centres, then lying and justification increase. If our state of being is high... operating from higher centres, then we would be able to catch our lies and the foolishness of justifying them.

I am not saying it is wrong to lie and then justifying it on the moral grounds, but it is of no use. It does not pay you in the long run. It is like mixing bread and mud. If we constantly observe, our higher states of being open up and we realise that if we continue lying and justifying, it is mechanical. This lying and justifying function like a machine. The moment we function like a machine, we destroy ourselves, as in essense, we are conscious beings.

I have a brother, who is very adamant and strong in his perception of himself and others that we have problems in dealing with him. Why is it so?

When we operate from lower states of being, our 'imaginary self' emerges. We imagine how life should be. Imagination thus becomes a reality. It deceives us. We see our imagination as truth. So, strong feelings and emotions relating to oneself and others are the result of this imaginary self. We have to dis-identify from it. We have to dismantle it. If one declares that one is perfect, one is a product of imaginary self. This is a part of self-lying.

If you observe that you are operating from an imaginary self, then make yourself flexible. Start seeing that there are many variables in life. Life is not so poor as to operate from one variable. This flexibility will break the rigidity. This will give a conscious shock to the mechanical imaginary self.

INSULATING ONESELF

Is spiritual practise a must for everyone? Or is it only for those who are interested in being spiritual?

One has to insulate oneself from the effects of worldly living. The environment has its strong impact. The external world is in a rat race ....of greed, of glamour, of respectability. It does not bother about real joy and purity. Naturally, external influence affects an individual. In this rat race even if one wins one continues to be a rat. Glamour gives you an illusory joy but your soul, irrespective of your colour or religion, needs to grow.

'Why does a fish in an ocean try to jump out?' asked a Zen student.

'The fish is trying to explore a world beyond the ocean,' answered the Master.

There is consciousness in each one of us like a fish that wants to explore into the unknown, wants to evolve and wants to grow. In order to achieve this, we have to insulate ourselves from negative forces similar to a plant being protected by a fence.

If you do not insulate yourself from negative forces, there will be a leakage of energies and that would hamper your growth. So it is necessary not to struggle in life and not allow negativity to control your life. One has to learn to float in life, to let go, let in the essentials and negate unessential feelings.

Can you give us an example to help insulate ourselves from negative influences?

For example, let us examine 'fear.' People live life in fear. It is out of fear that they worship; out of fear they get married; out of fear of insecurity they beget children. Whenever fear emerges, there is a leakage of energy. Fear creates a hurt body and it then tries to survive quoting philosophy and logic.

We try to protect ourselves from fear through the influences of the worldly life... by acquiring more money, more power, etc. But spiritually we can insulate ourselves from fear, only if we have trust.

Reflect on this.

We were very secure in our mother's womb, as our mother was taking good care of us. During delivery when we were pushed out into the world, all of us experienced as though we were facing death. We experienced tremendous fear. After being born, is it death or birth that marks our lives?

Trust that when one door closes, another door opens. Such trust insulates us from fear. The spiritual way of seeing is, if there is an impression or a negative impression of fear in the mind, one has to dis-identify with it. This detachment or dis-identification is the insulation that I am talking of. In *yoga* it is called *atma smaranam* - self-remembrance.' We have to remember to bring forth an impression of trust and dis-identify from impressions of fear.

What happens by insulating ourselves from a negative impression?

Worldly influences do not touch us, instead we would be in touch with higher vibrations and open ourselves for higher influences. The higher centres in us are constantly communicating something profound to us, but we close ourselves to them. It is like a cup turned upside down .... no amount of rain water can fill the cup. The moment we are available for higher vibrations, we attract nobler aspects of life. Our state of being attracts situations in life. Lower states attract lower aspects of life while the higher states attract higher aspects of life. This is the law of attraction.

When does devotion come into our life? Is it necessary to have devotion in our daily lives?

Devotion activates our higher centres. Devotion purifies our emotions. Devotion allows the finer vibrations to flow into our lives. Have you seen the differences between an Ox and a Dog? In India, an Ox is deployed for ploughing. It works very hard. An Ox undergoes a lot of torture. Its tail is cut to prevent it from swishing to ward off flies. It continuously experiences irritation due to the presence of flies over it. Because of this irritation, it works very hard. It is castrated, so that all it's energies are utilised for ploughing. When it becomes old and useless, the farmer either kills it or sells it for meat.

In the case of a Dog, it does no hard work like an Ox, but still the master loves it very much. Why? Because, a Dog showers love and gratitude. In return, it receives a lot of love. Just working hard is not enough. Don't be like an Ox. Learn to do everything from love and devotion. Be grateful to everything. Then our owner, the good Lord would shower love and blessings. This is the law of life.

With devotion, your third eye or intuitive eye opens, and you would see many meaningful co-incidences occurring in your life. You will see the mysterious hand of God blessing you.

Can you inspire us with a story in this context?

An arrogant man was announcing to the crowd that he had a perfect heart. He had just completed running 15 miles and was still in perfect condition. An old man struggling to get up said, 'My heart is better than yours.' The crowd was surprised to hear this. Then the arrogant man took out a magic crystal and peeved deep into the old man. The magic crystal revealed a lot of patches and holes on his heart.

'How can you say your heart is better than mine? You have many patches and holes when viewed in this crystal, whereas I have none.'

The old man said, 'All along I have used my heart, whereas you have not used it. Whenever I have given love, a part of my heart was given. Hence, there are holes in my heart. Many have given their hearts to me hence there are patches. I have used my heart, whereas you have not.'

The arrogant man realised his folly and said, 'Now take my love and my heart.' And in return, he got a hole and a patch in his heart. The perfect heart became imperfect but he made use of his heart.

Devotion purifies our emotions, opens the third eye, makes us recognise the meaningful co-incidences in life. Can you give a personal example from your life?

When we were building the meditation centre in Bangalore, India, we somehow managed to buy a piece of land. The construction at that time cost Rs. 15 million and we were short of funds. But we had trust. Our students hardly contributed. Someone, who we hardly knew, offered Rs. 3 million to start with. Then help came from many unknown sources. Had we focused only on people that we knew, we would have been disappointed. By being open to existence, support for a noble cause happens mysteriously. So don't get stuck in your ways.

What happens when our higher centres are activated?

One of my close student's husband was kidnapped. He was shot in the thigh. He was about 58 years with a history of hypertension and diabetes. He was covered with a blanket and was not allowed to move. After 4 days of captivity, he was saved miraculously. When I met him he was cheerful and consoling others. He told me that during his captivity he was chanting a mantra. In fact he was grateful that he was kidnapped and not his children. He narrated that he did not experience pain, despite a bullet passing through his thigh.

He was operating from his higher centre during those days. A great power opens up when our higher centres are opened.

Can you give us a technique to insulate us when confronted with a negative emotion like worry?

When there is worry, do not participate in it. Distance yourself from it. Just as how you would look at an object from a distance, see your thoughts from a distance and increase this distance. This will automatically reduce the impact of worries on you. Have you observed whenever you are sad, your thoughts and pictures are very close to you? Whenever you are happy, sad pictures either do not exist or they exist at a distance. Play with this experience.

So when you are unhappy, go on distancing your unhappy thoughts and pictures. Then simultaneously bring happy thoughts and pictures very close to you. Just by this, you will experience joy instantly. This is called as *sakshi* and *vikalpla* .... witnessing and imagination in *Yoga*.

Can you enlighten further as I am still not clear?

When you imagine a sexual scene, can you sense your body chemistry changing even though no one is around physically? What happens is, that thoughts and pictures of sex objects become very close to you, but your devotional feelings are in the background or at a distance.

Now imagine differently - you are in front of a saint singing devotional songs. Even though you are in the company of the opposite sex, nothing sexual triggers in you as your mind is filled with devotional feelings. Devotional thoughts and feelings are very close to you, whereas your sexual thoughts are in the background.

You get identified with one that is very close to you, thereby you experience it more intensely. Play with this and life will be different.

If you can go beyond your thoughts, it would lead to the ultimate fulfilment.

'STUCKNESS'
SOURCE OF ULTIMATE SUFFERING

I find my sister sticking to her point of view. If someone appreciates her, the best in her surfaces out. If some one finds fault with her, she is so self-protective and rationalising that in the whole process, she carries the pain of differences for long. That affects our relationship. Why is it so?

Rigidity is a part of identification. One of the important aspects of spiritual teaching is non-identification. If identification is our pattern, then we identify ourselves with everything. This identification is mechanical. Thus one develops rigidity and fails to see other variables in life.

One gets upset that one's point of view is not respected. This creates pain. The hurt body creates an imaginary self as a part of survival. This imaginary self has a great skill of justifying.... thus one gets lost in a field of vicious negativity.

Why do people carry the pain of differences for long?

This is a part of a mechanical mind. Unless we transform our mechanical centre into a magnetic centre, these negative patterns will continue. In my workshops, I wish the participants 'Good morning.' Then I question them as to how many of them meant the morning to be good? Most of them would have said it mechanically. 'Mechanicalness' is part of the mind where consciousness is relatively less. The more we bring in our 'presence' in whatever we do, the greater is the chance that consciousness would give rise to a magnetic centre.

Once a magnetic centre is opened in us, we see the foolishness of carrying pain. It is like mixing bread with cement. People are living miserable lives because they function mechanically. They are victims of their programming. One of my relatives who is a multimillionaire leads a poor life as he is unwilling to sell part of his property. It is against his concept of family dignity, but he lives a life of poverty. See how one can be a victim of one's programming.

I have received a great deal of knowledge from you. Is this enough to change my life?

There are two domains ...the domain of 'knowledge' and the domain of 'being.' Knowledge should be applied in life so that it enhances one's state of being, thereby one's life matures. Then from a matured being if one looks at the same knowledge it would have a deeper meaning. By applying the deeper meaning in life and in one's being, one's life becomes more mature and in the process, something very profound happens. Hence, knowledge should be applied in one's life or else knowledge would be like a donkey carrying sandalwood.

For example, one of the important teachings is 'to be more conscious.' Now apply this in your life. Be conscious of your body. Are you relaxed or tense? Be more conscious of your emotions. See whether your emotions mechanically hate someone or like some one? See your thoughts; see their compulsive behaviour. Become more conscious of your mind dominating you. Hence, practise being more conscious in your life. Apply it to your life. Don't make it a concept, as conceptual knowledge does not help.

Can you give an example where knowledge is just a concept, but not applied to life?

There are plenty. In the name of religion, there has been much bloodshed. Religion talks of love and oneness. Why then hatred? In Christianity, between Protestants and Catholics, so much of bloodshed has taken place. That God is all pervading is an important teaching amongst the Hindus, but why a caste system? Practically in all the religions, if you closely observe, there have been hatred and bloodshed among themselves and others.

How do we change the mechanical impact of life?

The mechanical impact of life can be changed through the teachings of the enlightened masters. On each occasion when we are forced to behave mechanically, let us bring the teachings of our masters to the fore. Through constant practise, a different dimension will flow. This is the dimension of grace. Then the third factor of grace changes our lives. The first factor is our 'mechanicalness.' The second are the teachings of the enlightened masters and third is grace. Grace can descend only when the teachings of the enlightened masters are applied consistently in our lives. Then the law of grace transforms our lives.

Can you please give us an example to deepen this understanding of how grace operates?

The 'mechanicalness' is to earn money by hook or crook. This is the first factor. Now if one practises the teachings of great Masters, one works on the principle that one has to earn money with good values; by right means. One should earn money out of love and not out of greed. This is the second factor. In this constant struggle to bring in the teachings of the great Masters in all walks of life, there will be an opening in which gracefully grace will flow. It is beyond one's known structure of logic. Something mysterious happens, an illogical factor emerges and one finds life to be fine and life will be prolific. Be open to the factor of grace. Grace operates not in a way you want it to be, but in its own way. Learn to appreciate the language of grace. God gives us what we need more than what we want.

Can you inspire us with a story?

An old man, disappointed in life, died. He was honest and could not tolerate dishonest people. When he met the Lord in heaven, he asked, 'If human beings are your creation, then all of them are your children. Why are there so many differences amongst them?'

God replied kindly, 'Each person who is born on this earth has a unique message to offer to the world. It is only through these lessons one understands life and Godliness.'

When people tell lies, it implies that *things are not as they seem*. The truth is beneath. Look at their facade. Their original face is behind their facade. Look closely at ones facade and discover their original faces.

When someone dies, it reminds us that nothing is permanent. Life is impermanent. So don't take life for granted.

When one criticises you, it teaches that no two people are alike.

When some one breaks your heart, it teaches you that loving someone does not always mean that the love will come back to you.

When someone cheats you, it teaches you that the root cause of evil is greed.

Even good deeds offer their own messages. Hence, the world is like a university teaching us in unique ways always. Let your life be one of learning, learning and learning.

When you unfold, it appears so simple and clear; but on leaving this place everything appears to be difficult to practise?

We are not individuals; we are a collection of many 'I's.' The 'I' that listens to me is different; the 'I' that creates problem is different. I am a father, with reference to my son, I am a son with reference to my father, I am a boss with reference to my subordinate … so I am multiple 'I's.

So every 'I' has to be transformed. Hence, it appears to be difficult.

In the 'presence' of a Master, the purity in him brings the best 'I' in you and you find the unfoldment simple. Without the Master's 'presence,' there are chances of negative 'I's emerging.

Buddha advised his disciples to move around with five seekers, so that one's 'presence' would impact the other. One's purity would empower the other.

It appears that we are forgetful and hence don't practise what has been taught?

Atmasmaranam ... self-remembering is very important aspect in one's life. We have to remind ourselves of the great teachings of enlightened masters. When we are forgetful, unconsciousness takes over. We have to become conscious and remember that we have to dis-identify with the wrong self. The wrong self has its survival games. We have to see them clearly and give a conscious shock with an understanding. We have to observe how the wrong self is a function of the 'lower self' and the game of life is to operate from the 'higher self.' This is not difficult, but one has to practise with joy. Don't work for joy instead work out of joy.

Man is not a unity of many 'I's' but multiple 'I's. Is this not a dis-empowering statement?

Truth is not dis-empowering. Whatever the truth, one should be able to see it. Truth does not operate in a way to please one. Truth reveals facts of life. Do you want to be with fact or fiction?

Further, we can unify all the 'I's.' That is the alchemy that spirituality invites us to taste. We can do that only if every 'I' in us is driven by a principle. We should be principle oriented. The foundations of our lives must be based on goodness. Every 'I' should be anchored on transformation. Transformation means growth. If all 'I's' are based on transformation, then we become individuals. Or else, we would be like those seated in a chariot with each horse galloping in different directions. Let all horses run in the same direction. Let all the 'I's' envision transformation. What a challenge! What a project!

ENLIGHTENMENT A QUANTUM LEAP

Quantum leap is a great discovery in the realm of physics. Electrons disappear from one point, appear in other points and between the act of appearance and disappearance there is no time gap. This is called quantum leap – a phenomenon described in Physics. All great discoveries from that point is known as quantum leap.

In the science of spirituality too, enlightenment happens beyond time. So enlightenment is not a process. Any process is within time whereas enlightenment is beyond time. Ignorance, which is a cause for bondage, can just disappear. In the field of consciousness, this is a great quantum leap. Let us be available for such a happening.

How can ignorance, which is a cause for bondage, disappear in the field of consciousness? How can quantum leap happen in the field of enlightenment?

It is not a question of how. It is not limited by logic nor defined by logic. But some explanation can be given as an indication but not as definition. Just as in case of physics, quantum leap can happen, so too if one has devotion with understanding, grace descends and one's ignorance just disappears. When grace descends, the impossible can become possible... like quantum leap appears impossible but is possible. For grace to descend, one's being should be filled with devotion. The power of devotion is beyond all logic. If you observe the lives of some of the saints, you will find miracles happening. For example, in the life of Kalidasa, a great Sanskrit poet, who was very dull and ignorant but when grace descended, he became one of the greatest poets in the world.

Is it true that in association with the good and the wise, one would be blessed with mysterious benefits?

A King invited a wise monk to his palace and honoured him. The monk spent a night in the palace as requested by the King. While lying on the cot, he found a priceless necklace and simply carried it with him the next day justifying that the King would not mind it. Subsequently, the monk could not sleep, as he was feeling guilty of his act. He then, went back to the King and returned the necklace.

The King felt the monk was joking, but the monk insisted that he had erred. The King enquired as to whether the food served to the monk was pure. The cook answered, 'A robber had stolen a bag of rice and on seeing the soldiers, dropped it and run away. We cooked rice taken out from that bag and served it to the monk.' The King at once said, 'This is the reason why the monk had thought it fit to rob me as the rice had 'theft-energy' in it.'

In India we are encouraged to eat food cooked by pure hands. This is one of the reasons, why food cooked by a mother is rated as the best.

How can one purify oneself?

People's ignorance is furthered by an illusion that when we change the world, we change ourselves. We feel that by changing the world we change ourselves. Change yourself first. Then you will not be affected by the world.

A King wanted to carpet his whole kingdom so that when he walked, his feet would not get dirty. His minister told him, 'Oh! King, why this cumbersome process. Cover you feet by wearing shoes and your feet will not get dirty.'

So change yourself. To do that, you should drop your past, you should not be imprisoned by your past. If you don't renounce the past, it would start defining you, limiting you. That you are a possibility will not open up.

Is it so simple to drop one's past? Past has defined me, past is my reference, so how do we renounce the past?

The concept of 'easy' and 'difficult' is very subjective. It may be easy for some and it may be difficult for others. Even if it is not easy, so what? Enjoy the difficulty. Treat it as a challenge. One finds it difficult if one does not understand that there are many layers of unconsciousness imposed on oneself... the layer of ignorance, the layer of social ignorance, the layer of religious ignorance. Layers after layers are superimposed on oneself. One has to uncover oneself.

A spiritual seeker needs to discriminate between what belongs to himself and what belongs to others. People around you are unconscious and they tend to impose their understanding on you. You have your own understanding. So you should discriminate clearly.

By negating what is superimposed on you, you will see yourself clearly. You may feel inadequate, as you don't have the benefit of the other's knowledge.

The whole crowd within you has to be renounced. You then start seeing yourself as pure and innocent; in the process a great purification takes place. Be silent and see how your knowledge is borrowed or superimposed. Watch them go and let go. See your original face.

Still I am not clear, what makes it difficult to drop our past?

You have to observe the connection you have with your past. If you closely observe, it is only a habit of being connected to your past. You have drawn your identity from ignorance and are used to it. It is just a habit. Any habit is hard to give up. Habits die hard. In the word 'Habit,' remove the H and 'a bit' remains. Remove 'a,' then 'bit' remains. Remove 'b,' 'it' remains. Remove the 'i' , still 't' remains. So remove the 'I'

See the influence of the past on you; is it a friend or a enemy? Is it freeing you or binding you? See the foolishness of it and just renounce it.

Renouncing the past helps in relationships. Is this concept useful in relationships or is it more of a spiritual concept?

Spiritual concepts can be applied in our daily lives. In fact, it has to be applied to our daily lives. For example, if you visualise your wife from the past, then the past would pollute the present. The past should exist as a reference but not as a limiting block. Your perception should be free to see her as 'she is' and not as 'she should be.' This is possible only if you renounce your past. The changes in her would never be visible, if you are operating from the past. Many relationships are messed up as they are controlled by the past.

'To know and not to act on what you know is equal to not knowing,' is what you have said so often. Why is that we don't act on what we know?

Knowledge has to transform into wisdom and only then, it will bless you. For that to happen, you have to practise. In order to practise, you have to remember what you have to practise. But we are forgetful and hence we don't practise. Self-remembering is the answer. In *yoga* this is called as *atma-smaranam* ... self-remembering. So remember what you have to practise. Keep remembering. This will eliminate one's 'mechanicalness.'

Can you explain a little more about self-remembrance?

In *Yoga,* there are four classifications.

Karma Yoga ..... Yoga of Action
Bhakti Yoga ..... Yoga of Devotion
Gnana Yoga ..... Yoga of Wisdom
Dyana Yoga ..... Yoga of Meditation

We have to remember and practise all of them.

Through Yoga of Action, teach your body to have a new movement. Every action has energy. Repetitive action has same movement of energy and hence leads to boredom. Through *Hatha Yoga* you make your body movements very different and experience a new energy. You train your body to be relaxed and vibrant. Move your body consciously. For example, in a sitting position, feel the energy of your body and better your sitting posture. See to it, you derive maximum relaxation and joy. Let every movement of your body have this awareness. This is the *Yoga* of Action.

What about Yoga of Devotion?

Every one has a feeling centre. Remember your emotions operate mechanically. Remember to separate them from your mechanical emotions. Create an inner separation from your negative emotions. Consciously choose positive emotions. The greatest positive emotion is devotion. Learn to consciously develop devotion. Anything less than devotion, negate it consciously.... like how you respond when some one sticks a poster on your wall, how you immediately remove it and then write a note 'stick no bills.' So too, in case of a negative emotion, immediately negate it and say, 'no more negative emotions.' Remember to bring in devotion in whatever you do. Adjust your emotion in a way you have only devotion.

What about Yoga of Wisdom?

Bring in more consciousness in your thinking. See how your intellect imagines and see its mechanical functioning. Dis-identify with your negative thinking centre. Remember to bring in more awareness and see what you can learn in a given situation. Adjust your thinking faculty in a way that it makes you feel young in learning. Let your learning make you feel relaxed. Let your learning make your feel you are growing and not burdened by knowledge. Remember them in all walks of life.

What about Yoga of Meditation?

Remember to keep your mind empty. See how compulsive thoughts are dragging you. Consciously be without mental words. Be in the present. Let your 'presence' be light. Remember to keep your 'presence' alive and light. Remembering all these aspects of Yoga is self-remembering …. *atma smaranam.*

Freedom
The ultimate gift

Are we really free? Is freedom a choice or bondage?

People imagine that they are free. If one looks at one's self closely, it would be clear as to how one is bound. Our lives are mechanical and we are not free. Most of our minds function mechanically... our perceptions, our conclusions, our all beliefs are mechanical. In this scenario it is a illusion to feel that one is free.

In order to be free, one's functioning has to change from the lower states of consciousness to the higher states of consciousness. One has to be magnetic. We are free to evolve, but if we are mechanical, we are not free.

Our inner nature is freedom. In fact, freedom is not the absence of bondage. If freedom is other than bondage, then freedom is bound by its freedom for it is free only in freedom and not in bondage.

Be conscious of your being mechanical; see how you are not free in your mechanicalness. You are free to see that you are bound. Let your centre come from freedom to see your bondage. Operate from that state of being.

Why are we not satisfied with life despite abundance in existence?

Even though existence is in abundance, man is bound by poverty. Generally people are not prosperity consciousness, but are poverty consciousness. People operate from scarcity and not from abundance.

We are not satisfied with life as our level of being attracts a particular kind of life.

One's life is like a small wheel and one is connected to bigger or smaller wheels. Life is interconnected. It is necessary that we disconnect from the smaller wheels of life and connect to the bigger ones. Learning to connect and disconnect is very important. The smaller wheel represents name and fame, money, power ... learn to disconnect. We are connected to them through our attitudes. There is a collective consciousness of small wheels and hence we are pulled by this consciousness into an abyss. Even wars are caused by these influences not necessarily by those who want war. The collective consciousness of small wheels has its own influences. These influences impact the sleeping humanity.

Living in this consciousness, one will be more a wanting being rather than a satisfied being.

Our willingness to grow impacts us, but does this impact the collective consciousness?

There is a principle called the principle of the ladder. Just imagine a ladder in which people are climbing. If one is unwilling to move up, it blocks others. If one helps the other to climb, one is not only helping oneself but also others. If everyone is disciplined, the process becomes smooth. If not, it is because of sleeping consciousness that one does not see the sanity of harmony and order.

If one is not ready to be awake, then one blocks another. If one is willing to grow, it impacts the collective consciousness and in turn it also impacts people around.

So it becomes necessary to make the right connection and disconnection.

How important is the role of a Master in the path of awakening?

An enlightened Master's being is awakened to higher levels of consciousness. His 'presence' has a rippling effect on others. He can see your blocks very clearly and help you open your inner doors. He would be a great help.

We have four doors to be opened. They are a conscious mind, a subconscious mind, an unconscious mind and a divine mind.

Conscious mind involves thinking, deciding, discussing .... which forms a small part of our beings. This has to be purified. Then the subconscious mind has to be opened. One has to have affinity to one's Master with a deep feeling of love and oneness. Even in disagreement with a conscious mind, a deep feeling of love opens the other's door.

The unconscious mind has to be opened through surrender. Surrendering to a Master can be a great opening. Surrendering involves considering the Master's teaching as one's breath. Let your agenda be dropped and allow your Master's agenda to guide you.

In other words, surrender your ego. Then the third door opens.

Finally, the last door has to be opened by the power of grace. When all the three doors are opened, grace will then flood into your being and through the third eye, an awakening happens.

A Master helps one to open these inner doors.

Is not surrendering, losing one's identity? Is this not dangerous?

There is nothing wrong in losing one's identity. Our identity is a sleeping identity. Our identity gives us more pain than joy. The illusion of joy is kept alive and the real joy is dead. It is worth losing such an identity. We give great importance to this identity as though it has uplifted us. Our identity is like a wave in the ocean with a disappearing importance.

Before surrendering, our conscious mind has to be purified. It involves right thinking. Through right thinking, the conscious mind knows and sees the beauty in a Master. This beauty does not involve only his knowledge but his being, his energy field. One will slowly see that a Master frees one from ignorance and bondage. One's being becomes light in his 'presence.' Only then, a layer of the conscious mind opens up. It is through these openings, one realises that surrender is in fact a surrender of suffering. By losing one's identity a different being opens up. One really becomes an individual, an indivisible being.

Should one suppress one's ego?

Can one remove darkness in a cave with the help of a bucket? It is not through action, but by light that one can do so. So too, by suppressing, one does not eliminate one's ego. It is by bringing the light of understanding that it is eliminated. Ego is filled with dreams. Dreams are not realities. You cannot fulfil them. It is like a mirage, it cannot quench your thirst. Ego creates illusions ...like a mirage, it makes you chase it.

In fact, there is madness in the world because of ego. Ego increases your desires. If you want to live, you need food but not name and fame. You don't have to be a great actor or a singer in order to live. But ego makes you feel that you cannot be happy, if you are not famous. It goes on creating illusions.

Through understanding, ego drops and not by suppression. Always find out what your needs are and what ego wants. Need is necessary, but the wants of the ego is unnecessary. Drop the unnecessary and live with the necessary.

> ***But management principles tell us to dream. They tell us life is wonderful with dreams and hopes. If there are no dreams, how can organizations survive? Has not material prosperity given us joy? I am confused.. Please elaborate.***

There are two ways of living life ... an enlightened way and an unwise way.

The unwise way makes one live life as a wanting being. The desiring mind has its own pleasures. Such a life will be filled with pleasures or sorrow.

The enlightened way of living involves being in the world of being and not wanting. One's body will go through the pleasures and sorrows of the world but one's being will be beyond them.

It is like you are in a house and you realise that it is not your house. You will not get identified with the house. You keep the house clean and even if it gets burnt, you are not burnt. The body is like a house, but the soul is you. You will not be identified with the body.

Whereas through foolish living, one gets identified with the body or the house. There is an ocean of difference between the two.

Your mind dreams but you are not identified with it. You may fulfil them with detachment. To fulfil a dream with detachment is a great skill. One has detachment because one knows that one has to leave all of them behind one day. The soul is not going to carry them with it. Ultimately the soul is detached as it leaves the body and its wealth behind. Look at your ancestors and successful people who are dead. They exist only in a photo. Only their photo remains but their soul is gone. So, be detached.

In fact attachment has created hell. Detachment gives joy. Detachment is not indifference but non-identification.

Fulfil your dreams with detachment. Learn this art.

Reflect on this story.

A King was attached to his wife and in the process was suffering. He wanted to find out if this was the plight of his ministers too. He shared his plight with one of his ministers. The minister answered, 'I am also attached to my wife and am suffering.' The King found out that every one of his ministers' plight was the same. The King wanted to know whether there was any one in his kingdom who was not henpecked and wanted to honour such a person.

Addressing a huge gathering, the King announced, 'All those who are attached to their wives, gather at the right side of the hall.' After a few minutes, the King found only one person still on the other side. The King was happy to note that at least there was one person who was not henpecked. He called him for the honour. The man said, ‘Please don’t honour me. I am here because of my wife’s advice not to join a crowd.’

WRONG STATE
A SILENT KILLER

What makes things good or bad? We are caught up in being either good or bad, can you unfold more on this subject?

The perception of 'good and bad' is not external. For example, a war is bad when it is fought with a bad intentions, but it is good when fought for a nobler cause. What makes anything good or bad is our intention. In fact good or bad are our states of being. If our being is mechanical, events around us turn out to be bad. We are conscious beings. Not operating from consciousness is like turning away from our basic nature. In such a state, our perception gets poisoned. Being conscious of our thoughts, feelings, opinions helps us see that we are not victims of conclusions that are pre-programmed. With preconceived notions our perception will not be objective. This leads to a wrong state. Any wrong state is bad.

Is it OK if I consciously flirt in a relationship as you say being conscious is right. Is there not something wrong in this chain of thinking?

You are a victim of your own logic. Can you see that you are dominated by your thinking? Be empty, be inwardly free from compulsive thoughts and see what kind of feelings emerge. If you are empty, free from your own logic, you will be free and such inner freedom will allow you to connect to your partner. Connected – not sensuously but sacredly. You see sacredness in her or him. This would make you complete. In this state of completeness, there is no need for you to flirt. When your stomach is full there is no need to eat more.

What is wrong in flirting? Is it not a beautiful sport?

Relationship is like gardening. If you plant a sapling under a huge rock, the sapling would die as its roots cannot penetrate deep into the earth. Relocating such a sapling would be meaningful. If you pull a sapling out before its roots go deep, and plant it elsewhere, there is a great chance of sapling dying, as you have not provided sufficient time for its roots to go deep.

Similarly give time for a relationship to go deep. If your relationship however comes to a dead end, then severing it is wise. To flirt is like planting a sapling from one place to another and not allowing it to go deep. There is beauty in depth, there is a shallowness in flirting. Relationship is not a game. It is very sacred. It is not like winning or losing in sports. It is a process where two souls help each other to unite, in order to experience a unified self.

Why does war exist? Relationship is like a mini war, is it true?

War exists because humanity is deep rooted in violence. What is within, surfaces. If there is love within, even if one is crucified, one can give love and say, 'Forgive them for they know not what they are doing.'

There are two processes taking place in most nations. Some are in war while yet others are preparing for war. It is because there is violence within humanity.

The root cause of violence is attachment. We are attached to our ideas, our opinions; we have become prisoners of our points of view. We don't have points of view, but points of view have us. We are so immersed in our points of view that we are attached to our points of view. If some one disagrees with our points of view, we feel hurt. We feel some one has hurt us as we have become one with our points of view. This hurt creates a hurt body. This hurt body wants to settle scores and retaliates with others. This whole game is nothing but violence. Putting an end to this form of violence involves not being attached to our points of view. Detachment gives rise to joy. If some one disagrees with our point of view, it is only a point of view. Understand this fully.

How do we put an end to a war in the domain of relationships?

If you treat differences as pain, then the differences in relationships will be painful. Then you feel the other is responsible for your pain and hence there is a war with the other. If two people have different points of view, it is only points of view but you are not the point of view! So don't be attached to your point of view. Your point of view is one variable and in the cosmos there can be other variables. Your point of view need not be the truth. It may be true to you but not the truth. Be bigger than your point of view.

The world remains almost the same but why does each one see things differently?

We perceive the world. This perception passes through our minds. If we don't know how to use it, we get angry, upset and irritated, then our minds turn as bad transmitters. In turn we become bad transmitters. Our minds should be pure. They must have a learning energy with an aim to grow. When one has toothache, even tasty food when eaten is painful. Not because of the food but because of the toothache. Similarly our minds being unique they perceive the same world differently.

So what should we do when we become upset and angry?

Be more conscious. Understand that a stimulus reaches our minds but we are not equipped to handle it wisely, then anger sets in. So be more conscious of how our mind works. Be more conscious of how we interpret a situation. Be more conscious of interpretation creating a problem. We interpret depending on our states of being. If our state of being is committed to transformation, then we understand how to use a stimulus and not be its victims.

What does it require to be more conscious? Does it stop being committed to growth or something more?

Being conscious means one needs to have commitment and observation. Observation is of two types. One is external and other is self observation. Science involves observation of the world of objects.

Spirituality involves self-observation, the world within. These two should meet ... science and spirituality. Science helps in changing the world through understanding while Spirituality involves changing oneself. To change oneself, we have to see ourselves deeply. We need to see ourselves without the seer. If we see ourselves with the seer, then the conclusions of the seer pollutes the seeing. Can we observe without the observer?

To observe without the observer which is self-observation appears more difficult than external observation?

Yes. Internal observation involves the subject.... oneself. The object here is also oneself. We are the objects of our observation. So the subject itself is the object. This observation is easy and at the same time appears difficult. It is difficult, if we are attached to our conclusions. It is easy, if we can separate ourselves from ourselves. Hence, detachment is a great discipline.

Can you explain more about 'attachment' through a story?

A monk was strolling on the riverbed in the company of his student. They saw a girl drowning. The monk rushed to rescue her and brought her to the bank. The student was just observing. After this, they both continued their walk. The next day during the monk's discourse, the student questioned, 'Was it proper for you, a monk, to touch a woman as we have taken the vow of celibacy. Is this not breaking the vow of detachment?'

The monk answered, 'I picked her up and dropped the thought that I had picked her, yesterday itself! I am surprised that you still carry the thought. Find out who is attached?'

We all live in one world but experience different realities, why is it so?

There is an external reality and an internal reality. External reality is a world of external objects. Internal reality is a world of thoughts and feelings. What makes a world different is the world of our thoughts and feelings. If you doubt your internal reality, ask yourself as to whether your feelings and thoughts are real. If you say, it is not, then you lack self observation. We experience the world more from an internal reality. What impacts our lives are our thoughts and our feelings. Observe thoughts and feelings that make us happy or sad. If something makes us sad, renounce it. Renouncing involves not being attached to your thoughts and feelings as they emerge. You give them a reality when you merge with them. The shadow becomes real if you get attached to your shadow. Detachment is the key. Detachment is not indifference. Detachment is being aware of the sanity of life. Attachment is insanity.

What makes our internal reality of thoughts and feeling so difficult to renounce?

It is our ego. We get stuck to the wrong 'I' in us. This wrong self is the ego. Ego exists in ignorance. Ignorance exists because of lack of observation.

WHAT CREATES MATURITY?

One has to bring in the light of understanding to all walks of life. When there is light of understanding, even death turns out to be a door to the divine. When one door closes another door opens. When there is light of love in your heart, silence in your mind and relaxation in your body, universal energy will flow in. In that energy your life will be a song of the divine.

A sign of maturity is when you operate from the 'higher self' and not from the 'lower self.' The 'lower self' is full of addictive thoughts, filled with likes and dislikes, dogmas and conclusions. The 'lower self' discourages you by creating invisible obstructions. The 'higher self' encourages you by keeping your mind empty; but filled with silence. Allowing the 'higher self' to operate is maturity. You experience a sense of ripeness. When a fruit is ripe, it falls from the tree. When you are ripe, your 'lower self' drops from you.

Am I an ordinary self or should I look at myself as extra-ordinary self?

We are born from a cell that carries with it the history of evolution and thus we are born as perfect human beings. This is cosmic intelligence. There is no real identity as such but we are more a flow of cosmic intelligence. As compared to cosmic intelligence, an individual over a period of time acquires knowledge through education that creates an identity. Such an identity struggles to be extra-ordinary through which uniqueness is established. Thus the ego is created.

Hence, remove the urge to be extra-ordinary, so that your 'self' will not be driven with an urge to be extra-ordinary. This is maturity. You can live an ordinary life with extra-ordinary awareness and alertness. For example, even drinking a cup of tea with alertness, love and liveliness, makes you feel extra-ordinary even though the act is very ordinary.

Why and how do we develop patience?

Patience is an expression of the feminine energy and assertiveness is an expression of the male energy. We should balance both in our lives. We need to understand the difference between patience and laziness. Patience is alertness while laziness is dullness. Patience requires energy while laziness does not. When there is patience, alertness results. One will be available to the rising sun, gentle breeze, twinkling stars... and there is no sense of urgency to reach out, but a deep energy that allows something to be let in.

Don't ask me how to be patient. Drop all the struggles and your attempts to be unique. Drop all the tensions that accumulate by questioning - 'How, when and why.' Instead learn to sit silently. You will find that the whole world of the stars, moon and birds are welcoming and entertaining you. Just lie down, see the vastness of space, feel the silence in the breeze and the warmth of the earth. Being aligned to nature, allow the mysterious energy to flow into you like Himalayan springs. You will soon discover that patience is God's gift to you. You will then develop the ability to float in the river of life.

I have become a stranger to myself. I feel like a foreigner to myself, why is it so?

In fact you have to rejoice in this feeling. When you become a stranger to yourself, something leads you to go within. If you feel you are an outsider, then something in you tells you that there is an insider. Learn to go within. When there are dust particles in your eyes, your whole body intelligence attempts to remove them. So too, your spiritual intelligence invites you to go within.

When there is boredom, be happy that something in you is inviting you to reach out to the more interesting parts of you. This is something similar to when we feel we are disconnected physically from our mother. This disconnection was a great gift and it was necessary for our growth.

This feeling of a stranger to yourself is necessary as it is nature's way to wake you up to go within. One has to make an effort to work on oneself not only through positive acts, but also through negative acts. For example, when a gardener digs, it is termed a negative act; but when he sows a seed, it is termed a positive act. Learn to use boredom to discover bliss.

Is the sought hidden in the seeker?

There are two types of accomplishments. One is the accomplishment of 'not-yet-accomplished' while the other is the 'accomplishment of already accomplished.' When you have to climb a mountain, it is an accomplishment of not yet accomplished. If there is a gold chain on your neck and you are looking for it outside by mistake then you realise otherwise, it is the accomplishment of the already accomplished. We seek happiness. But happiness is within us. In deep sleep we are happy; where did this happiness come from? It is within us. Whenever the mind is calm, happiness floods our being. With reference to happiness and silence, the sought is hidden in the seeker.

What should I do in order to be happy?

First drop your desire to be happy. Drop comparisons. Learn to focus on happy incidents in life and remember less of unhappy incidents. Mix with happy people. Drop the myth that aging is to be feared. Don't confuse material things as being equal to happiness. You may have all the comforts of life and still be comfortably miserable.

Don't allow your life to hang on any one aspect of life. Learn the many ways to be happy. Don't put all the eggs in one basket. Some people invest their whole life in a job and for whatever reason, when sacked from the job, they will be wrecks. Be like a wanderer at times. Learn to see changes in life as surprises but not as threats. Think less of people who bother you and feel more of people who care for you. Increase your wisdom and be happy. Your 'higher self' has all the answers, but the 'lower self' does not allow you to reach out to them, as it is rigid. The 'higher self' is a flow. Go with the flow. Allow the wanderer in you to sail in the ocean of life.

How can I stop thinking about people who bother me? They get into my blood and bones?

This is how the nature of the 'lower self' operates. The thoughts emerging from the 'lower self' always interfere with one's inner growth. Learn to put them away, like how a tennis player puts away a thought of an incoming ball as a threat. Renounce such thoughts. The *Veda* says, *'neti, neti''* 'not this, not this.'

When you have a hurt body, the 'lower self' will draw its energy from it. Renounce it. Create a bliss body. Just feel happy. After all, it is a thought. Thinking of an unhappy incident is also a thought. Thought is a word. As a negative word comes in your mind as a thought, just negate it. Don't give it power. Don't identify with it. Or just laugh. Start dancing and awaken your bliss body. Like how you avoid poisonous food, avoid negative thoughts too.

ADVENTURE
THE INNER GROWTH

Is adventure opposed to being spiritual? Is adventure necessary for an individual?

Man needs both security and insecurity. Insecurity is a masculine need and security is a feminine need. Both have to be balanced in life. I have seen rich housewives who are secure but something in them is dead. Something superficial exists in their 'presence.' There is no depth in them. The element of adventure is missing ... the masculinity. I have seen people who always look for insecurity and risk. They are uncomfortable by being secure. I also find some of them being imbalanced. Something is missing in their 'presence' too. It is essential to balance both masculine and feminine so as to be blessed with by one's own 'presence.'

The spirit of adventure has to be included in your life. Don't take this statement on authority. Truth has nothing to do with authority or tradition. Truth has to be searched for. In a search nothing is guaranteed. The only thing that is guaranteed is a beautiful adventure that helps you grow. In such an adventure, you learn the art of both accepting and rejecting. Then you would be able to filter many things in life.

If I am lost in adventure, will I not get burnt out?

Do not get lost in adventure, but find yourself in adventure. If you are getting burnt out, then something in you asks you to slow down. There is a God in us who speaks, but our mind is noisy and thus we cannot hear the divine speaking. When you are inwardly silent and addictive thoughts are absent, the silence and the meditative energies that emerge will heal you like medicine.

Then, walking is meditation, sitting is meditation, and drinking tea is meditation. Most often, the burnt out feeling is from your thoughts, which signal that you are burnt out. Bring a meditative quality in your thoughts. Watch out not to use mental words which are self-defeating. Bring in the quality of joy in whatever you do. Allow your actions to flow from the 'higher self.' The 'higher self' guides you when to slow down. The 'lower self' is rigid and unsupportive under the disguise of being supportive. Do not get cheated by its game.

Learn the art of easing and relaxing yourself. After a long run, sit under a tree, feel the miracle of your body, the dance of your breath, the music of your heart beat, the gentle kiss of the breeze... the quintessence is in being relaxed, being at ease with oneself. Whatever you do, let your centre be calm, silent and relaxed. Act from this energy field. Let action emerge from silence. The nature of your 'higher self' is silence, peace... while that of the 'lower self' is restlessness and ambition. See this distinction.

Is inner growth an art of inner flowering?

It is out of muddy water that a lotus emerges and blooms. It is still considered the queen of flowers. Similarly it is from muddy situations in life that the awakened mind arises. Flower gives fragrance unconditionally, so too let us operate from unconditional love. All great masters inspire us to live in abundance but not in scarcity. Be total and not fragmented. Live to the maximum and not to the minimum. Let your 'presence' reach others and shower them with fullness.

Real growth happens when you trust and operate from the 'higher self.' This 'higher self' is a flow, a learning being that enjoys the given moment in totality. Unfortunately, we trust our 'lower self' that is authoritative, rigid, and non supportive. It is a victim of likes and dislikes. Growth happens when you negate the 'lower self' and are centred in the 'higher self.' Your 'higher self' is an evolving being through which you come in touch with a mystic flower in you.

Can you elaborate on foolishness?

'What a beautiful baby girl you have here!'

'This is absolutely nothing. She looks better in a photograph.'

'Word is not the thing, the description is not the described,' said J. Krishnamurthy. When a master points towards stars, an idiot sees the finger. Word is a pointer pointing out the pointed that is other than the pointer.

Can you give us an example of our foolishness? How stupid it looks like?

Jack was taking a romantic walk on a bridge with his girlfriend - Mary. He looked at the lake and asked, 'What do you see there?

'The Moon,' replied Mary.

'My God, am I so great! How the hell did I go above the Moon?'

Similarly, we are drunk with words. Words have become reality to many. We live in concepts and words. We feel that a map by itself is a territory. We never see reality as we are a bundle of words.

Free yourself from words. You find the 'higher self' flowing in you. Look at the Moon without words. Learn to experience the joy of silence, which is the soul of the 'higher self.'

In adventure, one becomes courageous, is it not? What is courage?

Courage is an ability to be with 'what is' without being a victim of 'what is.' Courage is not an absence of fear. Do not allow fear to disturb your centre.

Courage is like exploring the unknown and not being a prisoner of the known. A courageous person explores the unknown with or without fear or in spite of fear, whereas a non-courageous person is stopped by fear. Respect what you know and have courage to explore the unknown. The courage of a spiritual seeker is different from the courage of a soldier. The spiritual seeker drops his mind and explores the heart .... it is a flight from the head to the heart ... has courage to accept even death as he knows the art of living involves the art of dying. By accepting death, he has accepted life in totality.

To accept both life and death gracefully requires courage. It is an expression of the 'higher self.' The courage of the 'lower self' is focused on winning and not accepting failure. The 'higher self' operates from a different understanding altogether. It views success as God's grace and failure as an individual's own making. Failure is a shadow of the ego. With this understanding, life becomes magical. The hidden secrets of life flow in us. One cannot succeed against the whole. One's success is the success of the whole. In fact one becomes the whole.

'You are the fullness. There is fullness, here is fullness. From the fullness, the fullness is born. Remove the fullness from the fullness and the fullness alone remains,' say the Vedas.

Yes, in adventure courage emerges. Let living be an adventure in the mystery of life. Life includes both time and beyond time. In sleep, you are beyond time. Learn to see yourself beyond time.

Lack of adventure makes us live in cages. Is it not?

A mental cage is mental imprisonment. A bird feels secure in a cage against its prey but the cage itself is a trap. It loses the joy of freedom and the vastness of the sky. The enlightened being soars in the sky of freedom.

Our mental cages can be 'Self doubt, fear of failure, greed for success, being jealous, should and should not, focused on the missing...' The adventurous spirit help us to free ourselves from the mental prison. The mental prison is an expression of the 'lower self.'

Consciousness A great purifier

The mind may be knowledgeable but it need not be intelligent. Operating from no-mind .... from the state of consciousness, one can be intelligent. The basic nature of human beings is pure consciousness. At present, our consciousness is identified with thoughts, emotions and body. We have identified with them mechanically due to ignorance. If one can see the body, mind and emotions clearly as 'mine' but 'I' am not them, then there is an awakening. For example, the shadow is mine but I am not the shadow. The dress is mine but I am not the dress. This understanding is a great purifier. The 'I' and the 'mine' are confused and in this confusion the 'lower self' emerges. Once we know 'I' is pure consciousness and this is only the watcher - the witness, we get into a state beyond mind. This is the 'higher self.'

What happens in this state of understanding?

The self without a higher state of understanding lives a life full of tensions. It is similar to someone stamping on our shadow and in the process we get hurt, as we have identified ourselves with the shadow. Our mind gets into a drunken state. We are burdened by the memories of the past; burdened by the projections of the future and thus we start living at our minimum instead of maximum. To live in the minimum is the 'lower self' while to live in the maximum is the 'higher self.' Once we operate from the 'higher self,' the dust of ignorance is eliminated. We will be clean and fresh. We will be in the flame of consciousness.

How do I understand 'who am I?'

I am only an observer and not the observed. The observer is a witness.

The witnessed is me but not the real 'I.' Suffering exists in me and not in the real 'I.' This is an important enquiry in Indian philosophy. The body is witnessed .... so the witnessor is different from the witnessed. The mind is observed and the observer is different from the observed. Feelings are observed and the observer is the real 'I.' So who am I? I am only an observer and to observe I must be consciousness, the awareness. This awareness has no form. If it were to have a form, it can be observed and anything that is observed is an object of perception. The subject is the real 'I.' So the real 'I' has no form and hence it is formless. That which is formless cannot be destroyed. Hence, Indian mystics say the self is indestructible. This has to be experienced and can not be intellectually grasped.

How does this understanding help us in our daily lives?

We live in illusions. We get identified with labels such as caste, creed, religion and nationality. We give up our lives for these labels.

These labels are just name tags, but we are not name tags. This understanding frees us from illusions. Most of our sufferings exist in illusions. Our lives chase illusions. It is like a thirsty man chasing a mirage.

How should I experience this experiential understanding?

By just being a witness, an observer. Let thoughts come and go. But 'I' do not come and go ... I am just a witness. Feelings come and go but 'I' do not come and go ... I am just a witness. Be a witness and don't get identified with thoughts and feelings. This dis-identification helps you experience a 'higher self' that is filled with love, silence and bliss. Then you drop your imaginary self, the 'lower self.' The seed does not know its potential. It should be willing to drop its seed-hood to become a fruit. The seed does not believe that it can become a fruit. The seed should have the courage to drop itself to explore the unknown. There has always been a danger due to infertile soil or rocks for the seeds, but it is a fact that seeds have survived. So too, there may be difficulties in dropping the 'lower self,' but our experience shows that enlightened beings have been and are around.

What is meant by SWOT analysis in management?

S - Strengths, W- Weaknesses, O - Opportunities, T- Threats

SWOT helps you to take sound decisions. Identify your Strengths, list them. Identify your Weaknesses, list them. Identify Opportunities, list them. Now foresee the possible Threats either by fulfilling or by not cashing in on the opportunities.

We should learn to weaken our weaknesses, strengthen our strengths. At the same time look for opportunities. Opportunities are always there but we need creative eyes to look at them. Now read this sentence 'opportunity is nowhere' - Some will read it as 'opportunity no where' and some as 'opportunity now here.'

Have wisdom to anticipate threats. One should have courage to face threats. At times people avoid facing danger. Their imaginary self does not want to encounter danger as it is addicted to dreams.

How do we weaken our weaknesses?

First, decide to weaken the weaknesses. Some people ask me, 'How do I make a decision? I am a poor decision maker.'

If you have not made a decision, then you have decided not to make a decision. Indecisiveness is also a form of decision. So decide first to weaken your weaknesses.

But how is it possible?

The 'higher self' enables it to happen. You just create an intention and leave it to the 'higher self.' The genesis of weakness is the absence of will. With a powerful will of 'I can,' change your thoughts. 'Can's' create success and 'Can'ts' create failure. So change your thoughts to 'I Can' weaken my weaknesses. Learn to be in the company of people who have weakened their weaknesses and learn their secrets. In fact, in their 'presence,' you will get inspired.

How do we strengthen our strengths?

Play a creative game. I ask my students, 'How many ways can you make use of a glass?' Generally the answer is, about 15 to 20 ways. Then I ask them to form a team and brainstorm. Invariably it will be twice or thrice the highest quoted individual number. In fact, an individual's best is less than the team's best. A team is always better than an individual. Apply this idea in strengthening the strengths.

Is there a real threat in achieving one's goal?

The real threat is 'You' – the negative thoughts, the negative beliefs. Unfortunately, we trust our doubts and not our creativity. We trust the 'lower self' and not the 'higher self.' Learn to trust that the 'higher self' guides you. Such a trust creates an inner temple, an inner church. Really temples and churches do not exist outside. One has to become a temple. Trust with gratitude. Trust that if one door closes another door opens. Your trust has the ability to solve the greatest of problems. But do not get lost in doubt. Generally one flies with thoughts of doubt but does not root for trust. Beware of such a state.

Develop a thirst for trust. When there is thirst for trust, a great energy awakens in you. The greatest threat is in not bringing forth such an energy.

When energy of trust is awakened, how does it impact one's daily life?

You will be in harmony with life. When in the midst of difficulties, you will not perceive them as threats. You trust all difficulties as divine surgery. When God gives you a problem it is to humble you and not tumble you. You will learn from your difficulties to become a better person and not a bitter person. You will be less of a thinker and more of an experiencer. You will be more in the existential domain rather than in a conception domain. When you are jogging, you experience the joys of the heartbeat and also the sweat rather than thinking why the heart beats and body sweats. From this field of experiencing the experience, you will operate from the 'higher self.' Your thinking from the 'higher self' is different from thinking without experiencing.

Ego
The Scripture of a Devil

The foolishness of modern man is in that an average man always thinks he is above average.

The Hindu scripture Bhagavad Gita quotes that it is easy to drop the ego and also mentions that it is difficult to drop the ego. Why is that so? Is it not creating a false hope?

The perception of 'easy and difficult' is the result of one's state of being. Swatting a fly is 'difficult' for some, while killing thousands is 'easy' for terrorists.

Dropping the ego is easy when we realise that we are less than a dot in this vast cosmos. It is foolish to live with the illusion that we are the centre of the cosmos. Dropping ego becomes difficult when we have this illusion. To live on hope is a symptom that one is not in the present.

But, is 'hope' not the breath of life? How can we live without 'hope?'

In any circle there is a centre and a circumference. If the centre of your life is hope then you will experience deficiency. If the centre of your life is enjoying the moment, living in the moment, being total in the moment .... then hope will be a circumference... then it is not a problem.

Let kitchen items be in the kitchen and bathroom items be in the bathroom. If they are placed elsewhere, then there is a problem. There is no problem with 'hope' as such, as long as it is in the circumference and not in the centre. Be alive to the present.

What is the nature of the ego? How does it affect our relationships?

The self with arrogance is ego. Self with the ignorance of who we are is also ego. Self filled with hopes and dreams is also ego. Ego lives either in the past or in the future, but never in the present. Its centre resides either in the past or in the future but it misses the present.

We are living in the world of ego ... the 'lower self.' But if our centre is gratitude and devotion, then we live in the present. Both past and future become mere reference points. This is the 'higher self.' The 'higher self' is a space from which possibilities arise. It is a flow. It is a learning energy. It is an evolving being. You have the choice to operate either from the 'lower' or 'higher self.'

When you operate from ego, your relationships will definitely be affected. Ego wants to prove its point of view. The point of view is more important than truth or happiness. In that state, you demand and not command respect. If a couple demands respect from each other, then they are beggars of happiness and not givers of happiness. In the egoistic state, an argument feeds the ego. Remember no one wins an argument. You accumulate more of bitterness and at different periods of time you settle scores with the other.

But when you operate from the 'higher self,' there is a healthy discussion. In discussion, truth is more important than who has said it. Happiness and well-being become more important than the survival of one's point of view.

Then a relationship becomes rhythmic. You enjoy being with the other and you enjoy being alone. You are neither dependent nor independent but interdependent. You share your joyous being and not beg happiness from your partner.

Why is it painful when a relationship breaks apart?

The identity of 'Who we are?' is created by what others have said about us. If others have told you that you are a great speaker, then you feel you are a great speaker. So your identity is the product of what others have said about you. So your identity is dependent on others. In fact others create your identity. Others validate you. It is painful, as you have invested so much on others. Your image is in the hands of others.

The fact is, the real 'I' in us is not created by others. The 'lower self' is a product of others, but the 'higher self' is our essence. The 'higher self' is a 'presence.' It is awareness. We have not learnt to operate from that state of being. Hence, we are alien to ourselves.

When your partner separates from you, you feel you are at a loss. Stop and look within. You find a 'higher self,' God waiting for you. Learn to discover aloneness in a relationship and beyond a relationship. Aloneness is not loneliness.

What makes relationships work?

- Operate from the 'higher self.'
- Operate from commitment and not complaint.
- Let your identity not depend on others.
- Don't settle scores with others.
- Create a bliss body and not a hurt body.
- Learn to expand others' comfort zones and not increase discomfort zone.
- Learn to convert a sexual act into a prayerful act.
- Create a learning and rejoicing family.
- Learn to be a good finder and not a fault-finder.
- Present your point of view and not 'poke' your point of view.
- Focus on togetherness and not differences.

When differences in relationship create pain, what should our vision be?

Let a difference be a learning point and not a fighting point. Let us rise above differences than be victims of differences. Once we start placing any difficulty in a sacred space we learn a lot.

A pencil maker gave a piece of advice to his creation – a pencil.

- Unless you are held by someone, you will not be useful.
  So too, we should be held by a higher purpose.

- From time to time you will be sharpened; but don't treat it as pain, only then you will be useful.
  So too, existence will sharpen us from time to time; don't be upset.

- What is outside is not so important as compared to what is inside ... a pencil lead.
  So too, what is inside in us ... love, silence, goodness ... is more important than the vanity outside.

- While using, the user may commit mistakes, but you have the power to correct and rewrite.
  So too, we commit mistakes, but we possess the power to correct and rewrite our lives.

- Wherever you go, you create a mark of uniqueness.
  So, like a pencil, let us leave our mark of goodness wherever we go.

[illegible]

[illegible] of our wishes.

[illegible]

[illegible] to be [illegible]

[illegible]

[illegible]

[illegible] to time you will [illegible] but [illegible] as pain, only then you will be [illegible]

[illegible] will shape [illegible] time to [illegible] up.

- What is outside is not so important as compared to what is inside [illegible]
  So also, what is inside [illegible], goodness is more important than the [illegible] beauty.

- [illegible] the pencil may commit mistakes, but [illegible] the power to correct and rewrite.
  So too, a human commits mistakes, but he possesses the power to correct and rewrite his mistakes.

- Wherever you go, you can leave a mark of [illegible].
  So, like a pencil, let us leave our mark of goodness wherever we go.

MEDITATION
THE ART OF OPENING ONE'S BEING

The word 'I' is the most common and also the most confused word. There is a 'lower self' and a 'higher self' in us. Meditation helps us discover the 'higher self.' The 'lower self' has many 'I's' .... I am a father, I am brother, I am the boss ... but these are only the roles that I play; but 'I' am not the role. Then who am 'I?' I am a space in which all thoughts and roles exist. This inner space is the 'higher self.'

This inner space is silence. Meditation helps you discover this silence. Silence is not the absence of sound but a 'presence' filled with life. Silence is not a product of thought but a space from which thoughts exit. When you look inward, you find your thoughts are seeking something in the form of pleasure, name, fame and power. The seeker runs after something. In the seeker the sought is hidden. Actually one is seeking silence.

There is no silence as long as there is the greedy self. The greed to become somebody and the fear of being nobody causes great stress. Silence is beyond thought and mind. The art of going beyond is the science of meditation.

We cannot go beyond mind as it drags us to the past and to the future, thus making us worry about the past and the future. It makes us feel the world of hope, the world of frustration and make us miss the world of the dancing present.

Why does this happen?

Our life is 'in time' and 'beyond time'; for example, in sleep we are beyond time. We experience only being 'in time' but we have not learnt the art of going beyond time, consciously. This creates incompleteness. Hence, we experience deficiency. This deficient self seeks sufficiency. This seeking makes one want more thus leading to a deeper state of deficiency.

The solution for this is Meditation.

How does one meditate?

- Sit in a quiet place. Just observe your thoughts. Let thoughts come and go, but don't get identified with them. Just be a witness.
- Now look for gaps between thoughts. You will see the gaps between thoughts as silence. The observer of silence becomes silence. You cannot observe silence from a noisy state. As you observe the

gaps, initial thoughts may be so many that you cannot see the gaps. Soon thoughts will slow down. Then you will see gaps and experience silence.

- Next observe your breath. Be conscious of every inhalation and exhalation.
- Your thoughts will further slow down. See and experience the warmth of air you inhale and exhale.
- Observe how inhalation turns into exhalation and exhalation turns into inhalation.
- Now just become silent.... without words. Experience stillness. In silence alone, true communication opens up.

How can we be meditative in all walks of our daily life?

- Through 'open eye meditation'..... do your activities but see that the noisy mind does not overpower you. Be aware of the fact that a worrying mind is an expression of the 'lower self.' Just do not participate with the worrying mind.
- Do not unnecessarily verbalise every experience. When it is necessary to verbalise, only then do it.
- Let your body movements be relaxed. Do not keep a tense body posture.
- Let your actions come from relaxation and let your actions deepen relaxation. Then such movements become sacred movements.

- Increase your feelings while doing any act. For example, while having a bath, feel the 'presence' of water; while you are walking, feel the breeze...
- Be aware of your intentions in every activity ... is it ego based or goodness based?
- Deepen your awareness in every walk of life.

When you deepen your awareness, you are in a state of meditation in spite of being in an activity.

How does meditation help in our pursuit of success?

One wants to be successful to be happy. Being aware helps you to focus your energies in the right perspective. Through awareness, a magnetic centre opens, while unawareness activates a mechanical centre.

Through deepened awareness, you will be calmer. Calmness inwardly makes you take a right decision. You know when to proceed and when to stop. Inner calmness is a great spiritual guide .... similar to homoeostasis - a balancing principal in our body. Silence is a wise principle in oneself. It is the expression of 'higher self.'

Can you illustrate through a narration?

A worker at his work place realised that he had not offered prayers that day. He forgot to bring his prayer book. He knelt down with a prayerful heart and said humbly, 'Oh, Lord, I have not brought my prayer book, but you are all-knowing. So I will read out alphabets from A to Z, as all prayers exist in alphabets from A to Z. Kindly put them together so as to form the right prayer that I do not remember.'

And the Lord said, 'Of all the prayers this is the best prayer.'

When there is inner calmness, some order will emerge. Some sanity will emerge. Meditation brings this silence.

What happens when there is no silence?

Firstly, your health gets affected. Unhealthy chemicals may be produced in the body. And your body may attract diseases. Disease means when ease is disturbed. Mentally, you always plan and in a state of preparedness even when not required, it creates a mental fog... tensions pile up creating a hurt body. This is called a subtle body in Indian scriptures.

With this, you will pick up unessentials in life and suffer.

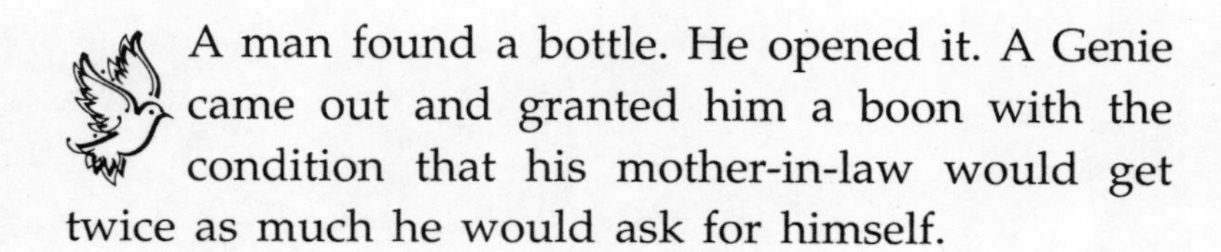

A man found a bottle. He opened it. A Genie came out and granted him a boon with the condition that his mother-in-law would get twice as much he would ask for himself.

'Now ask for three boons,' ordered the Genie.

'I want one million dollars,' said the man.

'Mind you, your mother-in-law will get two million dollars,' reminded the Genie.

'So be it.'

'I want a house in Hawaii.'

'So be it.'

'Now, I want to be half beaten to death,' stated the man.

We waste our lives asking for unessential and suffer. In a state of inner calmness, you pursue what is good for you and be awake to the good that is happening around you.

A priest asked, 'Why is it necessary to be quiet in a church as the sermon is being administered?'

One bright looking handsome boy said, 'Because people are sleeping.'

God teaches through nature and experiences. Let us not be asleep, but be awake. Inner silence creates wakefulness. Meditation is the art of being awake.

Meditation
The Art of Letting Go Sorrow

'To know' is the first step towards transformation. To know and not to act on what we know is equal to not knowing. So action is the next step. To deeply reflect and see the hidden meaning is *mananam* ...reflection. To be at peace with 'what is' and to be a witness to 'what is' is meditation.

If one is not at peace with 'what is,' then one is in conflict with 'what is.' This creates sorrow. In life one has to learn to be in harmony and not in conflict. Sorrow exists when one expect things that are momentary in nature to be permanent. This illusion leads to sorrow. To let go of the sorrow involves letting go of one's notion of things as being permanent.

An emperor visited India. He met a monk and asked as to how he could live eternally. The monk suggested a water body in the Himalayas. By drinking from that water body the emperor could become eternal. The emperor went in search and found the water body. When he was about to drink water, a crow on the tree cautioned, 'Don't be stupid like me. I drank water from here …. I am permanently a crow... '

God or existence in its infinite wisdom made impermanence not as misery but as a flow of change. To be with change and letting go of the addiction to be permanent is meditative living.

The essence of life is change but ignorance does not accept this fact. It prefers to remain in illusion. Hence, one experiences sorrow.

All that is needed is to raise the level of awareness and see the truth in 'what is.'

What do you mean by saying, 'Raise the level of awareness?'

See your body. See that you are not the body but an observer, a witness. See that the body is 'mine' but 'I' am not the body, like the shadow is 'mine' but 'I' am not the shadow.

The body is constantly changing. See the beauty in change. See the newness in change. See the surprise in change. Don't resist change, but learn to be in harmony with change. Enjoy the change. But don't cling to change. Bring this meditative awareness. Drop the myth that things are static.

See that the mind is also nothing but thoughts. Thoughts are like clouds. You are just like the sky, which is a witness. Thoughts come and go but you don't come and go, you are just an onlooker.

This witness is the essence of meditation.

But, is witnessing as easy as you are saying?

The perception of 'easy and difficult' depends on the state of one's being. Even if it is not easy, enjoy and play by practising being a witness. You find it not easy because you get identified. Identification becomes a pattern or a habit. Change this habit to not being identified.

Why does one get identified with many things?

Identification is the result of the negative energies in us. We call them toxins in our beings. This toxin exists due to wrong thinking or wrong living. Just intend that you will drop these toxins, these identifications. The power of intention is great. Intention is the mother of all creativity.

A great master was carrying a bag full of marbles. An evolved seeker recognized that he was an enlightened master and sought the mantra for wise living. He also asked him why he was carrying the burden of a bag full of marbles.

The master dropped the bag at once and said, 'This is my teaching.'

'What next?,' asked the seeker.

The master picked up the bag and said, 'Now having renounced, carry the burden. You find that they are just marbles, just instruments of play.'

Why is it so difficult to be playful as we grow up?

Society has sown the myth that it is the prerogative of children to be playful. As we grow up, there exists an accomplishment need in an individual. Society perceives that in the fulfilment of the accomplishment need, playfulness is an obstacle. Hence, one needs to be serious. To fulfil an accomplishment need, all that is required is commitment and not seriousness. Therefore, playfulness is impressed upon us as something bad. The wise approach is in being committed and still being playful. Do not be serious but be sincere. You will experience lightness in life. Your life will have more spiritual light.

Is playfulness opposed to being spiritual?

This is the other myth that one has to renounce. When you are playful, there is a deep sense of let go. Let go is learning to surrender to the flow of life. One has to ultimately let go of one's ego. When you are serious, you are in tension. Tension is the breath of your ego. When you are playful, you are relaxed. Relaxation is a part of being spiritual. Enlightenment is never in the future. Enlightenment is always in the present. To be playful, one has to be in the present. Hence being playful is an important door to spirituality. In India it is called *Leela - Krishna leela.*

Is physical pleasure opposed to being spiritual?

It is not opposed to being spiritual. If one stops only at physical pleasures, then one is limiting oneself. One has to go beyond. One has to explore psychological pleasures... music, fine art etc. Even beyond mind, there exists a different joy. One has to learn to go into the state of *turiya*... beyond mind.

The greatest medicine is meditation. The most dangerous disease is the limitation of the mind... world of thoughts. The highest madness is being imprisoned by the mind. The sanity is in going beyond the mind.

WRONG THINKING PUNISHES US

The quality of our lives depends more on what we are inside than outside. But how many of us really look within? Wrong thinking punishes us. Hence it is essential to look within and create an order therein.

It is very hard to look within. Why so?

We are programmed to believe that happiness is outside. We are products of such programming. Genetically it is ingrained in us that joy and happiness are outside. We have not introspected our lies. This lie or myth or programming governs our lives.

The process of thinking involves a flow of thoughts. Thoughts move outward in search of happiness, name, fame, money or power. Happiness however does not result from material affluence. It is a result of our attitude to life.

Happiness is a result of our being totally in the present. Enlightenment happens in the present. But our lives are always focused either on the past or future. Life is in the present. So be present in the present. Then a different 'presence' opens up. Whatever you are doing, be total in it. Bring in your totality of being in the 'here and now.' Then a different aliveness opens up.

Do wrong thoughts distort our relationship?

The most important thing is - can you look at anything without the interference of thoughts. When you are looking at a flower, can you just look? Pure looking is beautiful. But if you look at it from thoughtfulness, thoughts interpret it as a good or bad flower. A thought compares it with something else. By this you don't look, but superimpose. The discipline to look at something without thoughts is very important. When you require using your thoughts, only then should you bring in a thought. Try this out and see what happens.

When unnecessary thoughts pile up, they become pockets of energy. When negative thoughts pile up they seed negative attitude. Negative attitude enforces negative thoughts. These negative thoughts superimpose energy on the objects of thought. Thus the object of any thought appears to be negative. The influences that are created in life, be it in a form of war, politics, violence, is the result of the influence of negative energy that either becomes real or superimposed.

Our attitudes towards them connect us to them not as threads but as chains.

Breeding a negative thought is easier as compared to a noble thought. Why?

When your immune system is weak you are prone to diseases. Similarly when your psychological immune system is weak you are prone to negative influences. A healthy person attracts healthy people. A weak one attracts weak people. Negative energy attracts negative influences.

A negative thought requires no real effort. It comes from the lower mind. The lower mind is mechanical. Noble thoughts have to come from the higher mind; a more conscious mind. To be magnetic is from an upward flow, where as to be mechanical is from a lower flow.

How does a wrong attitude harm us? Can you give us an example to this effect?

A wrong attitude injures and harms us. We cannot live with a wrong attitude without harming us in some way or the other. A wrong attitude makes wrong connections. A wrong connection does not put us in the right direction. When we are not proceeding in the right direction, we are punished to that effect.

There is a male energy in a woman and a female energy in a man. Since we are progenies of both man and woman, both male and female energies are in us... they have to be in harmony. If we have a wrong attitude towards a woman, then the female energy in us is hurt. A disharmony outside is a disharmony inside. Similarly when a woman punishes a man, she punishes the male energy inside her.

When you create an external harmony, you create an internal harmony also. By loving a man outside, you love the male energy in you. When you hate a woman outside, a very important part of you, the internal female energy is also dwarfed and injured.

When there is right attitude, the wisest connection is made. This objective consciousness should include the subject too.

When we harm an external teacher, are we also harming the inner teacher in us?

It is very true. In us there is a teacher and a student. Our centre is a teacher teaching us in the language of silence, in the language of purity. The student in us should learn to listen to the teaching. When we do injustice to an external teacher, we are doing injustice to a part of ourselves. By respecting both a student and a teacher outside, we respect something in us.

Can you inspire us with a story?

James and Williams were friends. One day while walking together near the seashore, James slapped Williams due to a trivial difference. Williams wrote on the sand, 'My best friend slapped me today.' They later patched up and continued their walk. As they were watching the wonderful sight of the sun set in the sea, there was a strong current that dragged Williams to the deep waters. Immediately James rescued Williams.

Williams thanked James profusely and wrote on a nearby rock, 'My best friend saved my life today.' James was surprised at this and asked Williams, 'When I slapped, you wrote on the sand; when I saved you, you wrote on the rock.' Williams replied, 'My master told me that whenever someone hurts you, write it on the sand as it can be washed away. Whereas someone does a good act, write it on a rock so that it will be remembered forever.'

Williams continued further, 'This how one should manage one's hurt. Generally we do the opposite. People remember a good act like it is written on running water while a bad act is garlanded and thus keeping their hurt alive. This is poor management of life. My master has taught me to place both good and bad experiences of life in a unique way.'

the Sun set [illegible] there [illegible] dropped Williams [illegible] meet [illegible] immediately [illegible] Williams.

Williams [illegible] long [illegible] wrote on a [illegible] rock [illegible] my best [illegible] the [illegible] James [illegible] and asked Williams, When [illegible] slapped, you wrote [illegible] when I saved you [illegible] wrote on the rock [illegible] replied. My master told me that [illegible] you [illegible] the sand [illegible] away. Whereas [illegible] good [illegible] a rock [illegible]

Williams [illegible] for [illegible] small [illegible] opposite. People [illegible] good [illegible] the [illegible] a [illegible] Keeping [illegible] of life. My master [illegible] and bad experiences of life [illegible]

UNDERSTANDING LIFE

To know a teaching does not mean to understand it. There is a difference between knowing and understanding.

A man with 8 PhDs met a monk. He was proud of his achievement. Seeing his pride, the monk asked him, 'Why have you been so foolish in life?' The man said, 'You have misunderstood me ... I have 8 PhDs.'

'I have understood you; it is foolish to spend the best part of life reading instead of enjoying the birds, the stars and the moon.'

One may have all the knowledge but not clarity. One may know a lot and yet understand nothing.

What is that one has to understand about life?

Lack of clarity between understanding and knowing leads to confusion. One has to understand that one has many centres. There is an intellectual centre, an emotional centre and a body centre. In each centre, there is a mechanical and magnetic part. The mechanical part acts like a machine while the magnetic part acts with more awareness. One has to transform oneself. One's mechanical movements have to change. One's mechanical thinking should change. One's mechanical likes and dislikes have to change too. Mechanical emotions like jealousy and hatred have to be transformed. One can do this by bringing in more awareness. Then a complete being will emerge.

There is no greater force than awareness. When one increases awareness, even a poison can turn into a medicine and with no awareness a medicine can become a poison.

Why are we mechanical? When did this ignorance start? Why did it start?

Don't waste your time by asking 'Why?'

A King dreamt that he was a beggar. His *guru,* in his dreams told him the truth that he was a King and not a beggar. Now was he to argue with his guru or just wake up? The question of 'why' cannot be answered.

Tell me, when did time begin? You cannot answer such a question. Which came first an egg or a hen? There is a logical fallacy in the very question. Realise that we are mechanical. Bring in more awareness and see the transformation of life. Even inert objects have life. With loving awareness treat any object and it will guide you mysteriously. Your intuition and purity have to increase to receive this message. When you bathe, lovingly talk to water. When you sleep, with loving awareness talk to your pillow and a divine connection happens. Let these not be mere words, but with complete feelings. Memorising words is just not enough.

What is an understanding that one should have in a husband and wife relationship?

What are the differences between a pair of eyes and a camera? If capturing an image is the purpose of the eyes, then a camera will do. Eyes are meant to see the divine. Eyes are meant to see beyond forms, like a sculptor sees an idol in a gross stone. So too, eyes are meant to see the divine. A relationship is meant to see the truth. Hence, marriage is a commitment and not a convenience.

There are differences in a relationship. Do not give too much of importance to them. Give importance to your love and commitment, to your commonality, like you enjoy the joy rides in an amusement park, even though it appears scary. It gives you jitters but still you enjoy. Enjoy your relationship.

It is said, 'Do not judge.' Is it easy not to judge? In a relationship, is it not necessary to judge?

Keep yourself relaxed. Increase your awareness and love. Not to judge should not be a conclusion. Don't make it as a demand or compulsion. Let there be a choice. There is a difference between 'should' and 'choice.' 'Should' create stress and limits you to only one option. Choose not to judge. It is not a demand but a wise choice.

The danger of judgement is that you stop seeing the object of judgement and you are more in your judgement. In life, you have to make judgements, but don't be a victim of your judgements. Suppose, a thief enters your house, you have to judge him but then, be open to the possibility that he can change. Assume, you meet him after ten years, see if he has changed or not. Do you still judge from the memory that he had been a thief? If you do not have this awareness, you will not see the change in a person even if he has changed.

Can you give another example of what one should be really aware of?

Negative emotions poison life. Like avoiding poisonous food, avoid negative emotions. Like how you are very alert when you see a poisonous snake, be very aware and alert of negative emotions. Let them come, don't identify with them. Don't participate in them. Choose to create a new will, not be driven by negative emotions. They deplete your energy. They keep you asleep. They are harmful and heavy. They make your life complicated. For example somebody's success should not be your failure. We define our failure by somebody's success. We feel jealous seeing someone successful. Jealousy is a great poison.

Can you elaborate on your statement 'Let not somebody's success define your failure?'

If you go on comparing, life becomes miserable. If somebody is better than you, learn from them; enjoy others' success. No one can have all the good qualities. Someone will always be better than you at some level. Do not whip yourself with this comparison. Instead get inspired by someone's success. Learn to validate yourself wisely. Compete with your potential. Even if you compete with others, enjoy it. See the beauty all around. Do not define your success and failure by someone's success and failure.

RELAXING TENSIONS IN LIFE

Why is there so much of greed for sensation? Should I renounce sensation or indulge in it?

When one is in a state of tension for a long duration, there is an inner void. This void or inner incompletion is like dust in your eyes. Your effort is to remove the dust from your eyes, as it is alien to your body. Similarly, incompletion is alien to you and it is natural that you put effort to remove it.

You attempt to remove inner incompletion through indulgence. You feel different sensations would give you completion.

The greed for sensations increases incompletion. The desire for more and more, makes you a wanting being rather than a complete being. During sleep there is no wanting, as you are complete.

Please understand that it does not mean condemning your sense organs. Keep them alive and pure.

You must realise that sensations are fine as long as you do not get addicted to them. An addiction happens in ignorance. Such ignorance spills through sense organs too.

How do we relax tensions in life?

Learn the art of balancing life. Do not put all your eggs into one basket. Learn to open your body centre through exercise, yoga, deep breathing.... learn to open your mind. There is joy when you learn and when you keep your mind open to new possibilities. Learn to open up your bliss centre.

Reflect on this.

A Prince met Lord Buddha. Lord Buddha's 'presence' and 'being' inspired him to be a monk. The Prince was a great musician and led a luxurious life. After initiation, he went to the other extreme. He renounced everything. He started fasting vigorously and walked on thorns. Buddha enquired, 'If the strands of the guitar are very loose, can you play good music?'

'No,' replied the Prince.

'If the strands of the guitar are very tight, can you still play good music?'

'No,' replied the Prince again.

'Don't go to extremes, it only through right tuning of the strands that you can play good music. Similarly balance your life well and automatically music would flow into your life,' advised Lord Buddha.

What steps do I take in order to relax tensions in life?

Mostly, tensions emerge from the way your mind languages your experience. For example, a student runs several miles and enjoys running but when it is made a punishment, running creates tension. Where does the tension come from? It is through the interpretations in one's mind.

Observe a surfer.... the stronger the waves, the more does he enjoy it. He decides that he is going to enjoy the waves while surfing. When waves are strong, he is totally present in the moment. There are no interfering thoughts in him. In such space something in him makes him very alive to the life around him.

Learn to be in the present. Be aware of the present in total. There is joy being in the present. Do not get lost either in the past or future.

Learn to live from the 'higher self' and not from the 'lower self.' The 'higher self' encourages you, as it is filled with positiveness. The 'lower self' is an interfering self. It discourages you. It acts more like an obstacle.

Learn to relax your body. Learn to relax your mind. When thoughts emerge, see them as a wonder. See the beauty of your thoughts. Do not fight with them. See them like a play.

Slowly you create a synergy with your thoughts.

Whenever possible, be without thoughts. Learn the art of being empty. Do not verbalise an experience. Thus your mind relaxes.

Is there a difference between an ambitious attitude and a meditative attitude?

Yes. There is a difference. It is like darkness and light. Ambitions keep us always in a whirlpool of tensions with the hope that we will be happy. It wants us to be like others. Or it wants us to be better than others and in the process one becomes bitter.

Can my house be like that of a rich man? Or can my house be better than that of my neighbour? You are always lost in comparison. But life is simple. Ambitions make it complex.

Only if you stop the greedy game of going ahead of others, can you be happy.

A meditative attitude is very different. Meditation awakens your awareness. Once your awareness is of high order, you realise the foolishness of comparison. You would not allow others' success to define your failure. You would see the beauty of 'what is' and not get lost in 'what should be.'

You would see the uniqueness of yourself. Everyone is unique. Everyone is incomparable. You would learn the art of seeing beauty even in imperfection. You would participate in the miracle of life than being busy in judging life. You would listen to the music of life. You would listen to the *mantra* of life or the song of life. Your listening would be with your heart. Without this inner and outer, music will not be heard. With this, your perception awakens to newer heights.

Learn to look at life differently.

Listen to the song of life.

Listen to the music of life.

Let your heart open and bloom.

Let your perceptions see the glory of the moment.

Let your life be the song of the divine.

Learn to look at your difficulties as divine surgeries.

Learn to convert your worry into wisdom.

Learn to convert frustration into fascination.

Learn to be more happy than right.

Learn to be a wise parent.

Learn to make your marriage a miracle of togetherness.

THE HIGHER SELF
A FLOW OF COSMIC INTELLIGENCE

What is your message for the New Year?

Let the New Year bring you the depth of devotion, humility and understanding. Life without understanding, humility and devotion has no substance or depth. Acquire these three qualities through effort and prayer. Let your efforts have prayerful attitude. With prayer in one's heart, one will know how to surrender and allow God to play the game in one's life.

Reflect on this example.

Jesus, Moses and an Old man were playing Golf. Moses hit a ball that passed through a huge pond. The pond gave way. The ball fell on the other side. Then Jesus hit a ball that passed through the pond. Here again the pond gave way. There was a small hillock after the pond. Even the hillock gave way and finally the ball landed on the other side of the hillock. Now it was the turn of an old man. When he hit a ball, the ball got stuck on a huge tree. There was a strong breeze, which made the ball to fall into the pond. A frog in the pond caught the ball. A snake caught the frog. An eagle watching from the tree top, caught the snake and flew away. In between the eagle dropped the snake from its clutches... the snake in turn released the frog... the frog released the ball. The ball fell right on 18th hole of Golf course. Moses looked at Jesus and said, 'Never play golf with this old man.' The old man was none other than Jesus' father, Jehovah, the Lord.

Look carefully at this example. When Jehovah, the Lord played the stroke, the breeze, eagle, snake, frog, pond….. helped mysteriously. When you surrender, mysterious forces start helping you in reaching your goal. You have to put in effort, but with deep prayer. You will find invisible, mysterious forces help you. With an attitude of surrender and prayer in one's heart, a prayer enhances quality of surrender.

Let your devotion have depth and understanding. When you have an understanding, you will have depth. When there is humility, life becomes extremely rich.

Why should there be humility in life? It is out of ego that we are successful. Isn't it so? Is not humility an obstruction to success?

This is an ordinary way of looking at life. It is not the ego that takes you to your goal but it is your commitment. A commitment born out of understanding will enable you to reach your goal. Ego only creates pressures. Ego creates stress. Ego is an arrogant 'I.' It is an 'I' that has no sacred understanding. When there is humility, one still has 'I,' but the 'I' has understanding, a deep understanding that the ingredients of success are not only variables of one's effort, but also a variable called grace. When there is humility, one understands that one of the variables is effort, but there are several invisible forces that help one. One develops gratitude towards those invisible forces. Through gratitude, humility emerges. In humility, 'I' does not demand instead 'I' expresses thankfulness.

What creates tensions in life is 'I' in the form of ego that is always demanding. Such demanding nature of the ego creates tension... and tension does not allow one to even enjoy success. An egoistic person even if successful, cannot enjoy his success. It is similar to a person having a toothache and not relishing a good dinner. An egoistic person does not enjoy his success totally as his ego develops loads of arrogance. But when a humble person tastes success, he would be grateful. When he is grateful, he wholly enjoys his success. In a thankful space, one would be bestowed with an ability to enjoy the miracle of one's success. And such a person will include in his perception all those invariable forces that contribute to his success.

Where is the time for one to practise deep breathing exercise and meditation, even though one appreciates the benefits of them. What should one do?

If you are on a flight, particularly in the international sector, you would find that breakfast, lunch, dinner are served to about 300 people... just imagine the spatial intelligence to store so many items. Similarly, if a person can have the benefit of spatial intelligence, he would have time intelligence to optimise time wisely. Therefore, Time Management is a very important aspect in your life.

A Commander-in-Chief was fighting with swords held in both his hands. An R&D person intervened and told him that he had invented a gun that could be useful in place of swords. The Commander-in-Chief till then had not heard the word 'gun' and retorted, 'Don't disturb me. Can you not see I am busy fighting my enemies?'

Is this not ridiculous? A gun is definitely more useful in a fight as compared to the swords. But, the Commander-in-Chief was so busy and immersed in his fight that he had no time to study what was useful and what was not.

Look at the SWAP Technique, a powerful technique.

'S' means Stop,

'W' means withdraw and watch,

'A' means Analyse,

'P' means Proceed Positively.

The Commander-in-Chief in the above example could have adopted this technique for his benefit. SWAP also means exchange of energies. So we should always stop, withdraw and watch, analyse and proceed positively. In life too, please apply this technique. Stop now. Withdraw and watch. Analyse. Proceed positively. And you find time wasters, which you can comfortably eliminate. Time intelligence is as important as spatial intelligence.

How do we develop enthusiasm in life?

It is a very important aspect in life. Study the life history of successful people and you would find that one of the ingredients was tremendous enthusiasm or the passion to live life. One should have passion to live life. It is said, Edmond Hilary who climbed Mount Everest, failed thrice earlier. Later at a party hosted in his honour in New Zealand, he looked at the portrait of Mount Everest and humorously remarked, 'Mt. Everest has a problem. The problem is, it cannot grow more than about 29,000 feet, whereas I have the ability to grow in my ability to climb Mt. Everest.' What he meant was that he has the ability to grow whereas Mount Everest stood at the height of about 29,000 feet. Look at his passion. In the very next attempt, he scaled Mt. Everest successfully.

What is the secret of successful people's enthusiasm?

In us there is a 'lower-self' called *Jeevatma* and a 'higher-self' called *Paramatma*. One can either operate from the 'lower self' or from the 'higher self.' When one operates from the 'lower self,' one finds his life is not powerful whereas operating from the 'higher self' results in the opposite. This is the choice before us.

If one operates from the 'lower self,' life opens up as a threat. While operating from the 'higher self,' the life opens up as opportunity. Operating from the 'higher self' consistently generates enthusiasm.

Why does such a thought emerge wherein I look at the external situation as a threat?

Any situation viewed as threat is an example of one involving the 'lower self.' The 'lower self' operates as an interfering thought or an obstructing thought. The 'higher self' operates as a supporting thought, not as an obstruction. In any situation in life, if seen as opportunity, it is supportive. If seen as an obstruction, it is like a danger or a threat.... it is a function of the 'lower self.'

Our bodies have an immune system; if it is weak, the body is prone to disease. So too, we have a psychological immune system. If our psychological immune system is weak ... we are upset, hurt, frustrated. Like genes in our bodies, our minds are also products of evolution of many years. When our psychological immune system is weak, we are prone to perceive external situations as dangerous or as obstruction. It only calls for strengthening the psychological immune system so as to be powerful individuals.

How do you make it powerful? Like how we make the physical body powerful by right exercising and dieting, so too, the psychological immune system can be made powerful by not allowing the 'lower self' in us to operate... instead we should encourage the higher centre to operate in our daily lives.

I am still not able to distinguish between the 'lower self' and the 'higher self.' Can you elaborate?

We are born from a single cell. This cell carries in it the evolution of intelligence in abundance. This cell is born as a perfect cell and has evolved itself as a human being. We have not taken birth as a rat, a cockroach, or a lizard. We have taken birth as human beings. So this cell carries in itself the evolution of intelligence and carries with it the history of evolution too. Further, this cell has the capacity to split into many cells and thus help in reproduction.

How would you rate such a perfect cell on a scale of 1 to 100? Generally it is 100. Don't be so generous and rate it at, say 98.

A child born from such a cell, grows into a man, studies and obtains PhD in a life span of 45 years... acquires vast knowledge. How would you rate the acquired knowledge as compared to knowledge associated with the cell evolution? Generally it is rated at about 2 or 3 on a scale of 1 to 100.

In our lives we operate from acquired knowledge, rather than the cosmic intelligence of the cell.

Where do we draw our identify from? Most of us draw our identify from our acquired knowledge. Don't we? Why is it so? Because through acquired knowledge, our ego is established, our identity is established, our address is established. Whereas in cell intelligence that we have not created, but are gifted with, our uniqueness is not established. Ego is established in the 'I.' The acquired knowledge is the 'lower self.' The knowledge from which we are born – the cell evolution is the 'higher self.'

Let us draw our identity from this growing cell that is the 'higher self.' But alas, we don't trust this. Instead we trust our acquired knowledge. In life we should eliminate our 'lower self' and operate from cosmic intelligence. The acquired knowledge will be supportive in our growth and not obstructive. Understand this distinction.

> ***Do you mean to say that we should not acquire knowledge? The 'lower self' should not exist?***

Acquired knowledge should support the 'higher self,' not obstruct it. For example, in a game of tennis, when you see a ball coming from an opponent, your thought should not interfere with it and obstruct your spontaneous effort to hit a ball. But if you think, 'Oh, I am going to miss it because my history of missed stroke last time'; then acquired knowledge is obstructing. As a player, you cannot succeed.

Suppose, the 'higher self' looks at a ball in a different way - "With a focused awareness I allow my being that has evolved to guide me in hitting a ball. In case I miss it, the 'higher self' being a learning and evolving being, makes required corrections the next time I face a ball... but whereas acquired self or the 'lower self' creates an image that I am not good and I am not lucky. This image makes me look at a ball next time as a threat and acts as an obstruction. The 'lower self' is rigid, while the 'higher self' is flexible in learning and growing. I will not allow my static conclusions to decide my action instead allow my flow to decide a response."

How do we apply this understanding in our lives?

For example, take a game of tennis. Don't allow interfering thoughts to say that you may miss the ball while playing a game. Your boss may be a problem. But don't look at him as an obstruction. Don't look at him as nuisance. Instead look at him from the 'higher self.' When you look at him from the 'higher self,' the intelligence guides you to handle him. Whenever a thought is interfering or obstructive, eliminate it instantly and operate from your being... you will learn to enjoy handling situations in life. Always learn and let your living be based on the 'higher self...' as an evolved being, that has undergone many creative processes of evolutions.

If creativity emerges from the 'higher self,' how can I be creative as I am only a telephone operator?

Learn to trust the 'higher self' which is an evolving learning being, but we trust acquired knowledge... the ego and doubt the 'higher self.' We have to learn to trust the 'higher self' and discard the interfering self. Any creativity emerges from the 'higher self.' We have evolved, as human beings which itself is a part of creativity. We need to trust that process.

If you are a telephone operator what should you do?

My advice is when you pick a call, play the awareness game. Operate from the 'higher self.' Don't operate from the 'lower self' and tell yourself that it is a boring job. When you pick a call, rate the voice, the level of affinity, the level of liveliness, the level of irritation, the level of tone modality, pause, pace, pitch, punctuations, voice modulations... on a scale of 1 to 100... play it like a game, and note down. Now, also note down your response with respect to each of the above parameters.

Let your response have a higher level of affinity, liveliness and tone modality. And see how you can enhance these on a consistent basis and rate yourself on a scale of 1 to 100. Creativity can reach higher pinnacles even in routine activities. For example, a musician with the simple seven notes spends his whole life in mastering his art of music and creates masterpieces in music. The point is to treat each activity as a game where even replying to a telephone call can be interesting and exciting.

THE WISDOM OF A WISE RAT

Let us not brand anybody as good or bad. If one operates from the lower state of consciousness, then one's actions may not be proper. This is called the *Tamasic* state in Sanskrit. If one operates from the higher state of consciousness called *satvaguna,* then one's actions may be different. The Gita says our inner states are constantly changing. Therefore, depending upon the state of being that we are in, our inner states co-relate to our actions.

If a person has indigestion and is vomiting, no amount of control can help; mere advise to stop vomiting will also not do. If one is operating from the lower state of consciousness, one's actions will be a reflection of the 'lower self.'

We, therefore, should constantly look at our behaviour, look at the states we are in, within. This also helps us in softening the other's inappropriate or erratic behaviour. The erratic behaviour may be due to their states of being.

More than any amount of attitudinal change, it is behavioural change that enhances the quality of life. Let us not get deceived by patting ourselves that we possess a good attitude. Unless it results in behavioural changes, there is no real change. Behaviour change alone brings about true change.

The Gita encourages us to be calm and serene irrespective of the situations that we face in life. Only such an individual is closer to enlightenment who remains calm. The greatest discipline is in keeping our minds calm in spite of external turbulent situations. This is the core teaching of the Gita.

A Zen Master was asked about the secret of his being always happy. The Zen Master replied, 'When I wake up in the morning, I ask myself whether I want to be in heaven or hell? Then I decide to be in heaven. The moment I decide to be in heaven, I create heaven in every moment of my life.'

If you want to be happy, first decide to be happy. Ultimately it is your decision. And the moment you decide, things will be very different.

Can you explain the Law of three in esoteric teaching?

The Law of three is a beautiful esoteric teaching. The first law states that you put your effort .... it is called 'A' force. Every action has equal and opposite reactions. The moment you put positive action, invariably a negative force will come into picture …but, you tend to give up quickly. You give up your endeavour to be positive. Then a second force …. 'B' force comes into focus. If you continue to put in efforts, then the third force … 'C' force will descend and support the effort … 'A' force.

Therefore it is said that Grace will descend …. what we perceive as negative will start supporting our endeavour to be positive. Until that time we need to have patience and perseverance.

For example, in Hindu mythology, there are umpteen narrations where a ritual of sacred fire is performed for a noble cause. Invariably, we find that negative forces in the form of a devil comes in the way of performing a ritual of the sacred fire successfully. But, the performance of a ritual of sacred fire continues. It is very symbolic. In life too, one can apply the principle of the Law of Three …. be it in relationship, family…

How can we live successfully amongst our enemies?

The choice in our life is either we come from commitment or complaint. We have to decide that. Invariably we find people who are powerful are those who operate from commitment. And those who are powerless, always operate from complaint. One's state of being will be powerful if one operates from commitment.

Another dimension one needs to add is to operate from selflessness. When we do something that is selfless, we find unknown forces mysteriously strengthen our hands. *Pathanjali,* a great Yogi says, 'Do something good ... be in the path of goodness, and... you will find forces that mysteriously help you.'

We look at life from our structure of thoughts and therefore, find the world as imperfect.

Let us learn to operate from what is beyond our own selves. A selfish person never understands the language of the selfless person. Every Monk is invariably criticised or even crucified because all enlightened masters wake up people from their slumber, which is seen as disturbing.

There was a rat and a wild cat. Both were wary of each other. The rat inside its hole was cautious about the wild cat waiting outside and the wild cat too was waiting for its catch. This waiting game continued for long. Then the wild cat lost its patience, started strolling and got caught in a hunter's net. It was struggling to break free. Realising this, the rat came out and went around the net happily.

At that time, the rat saw a huge bird charging towards it. The rat had no time to get back in to the hole. Being a smart rat, it struck a deal with the wild cat, 'You help me and I will help you.' Then the rat went inside the net and sat on the lap of the wild cat. The bird had a unique sight of the rat sitting on the lap of a wild cat and it also realised that its efforts to catch the rat were futile and left the scene in vain. The rat then came out and told the wild cat that it would honour its word and started cutting the net very slowly. The wild cat became impatient and retorted at the rat,' You are intentionally cheating me. I promised you that I would not harm you. I will honour my word.'

The wild cat did not understand the rat's strategy. A hunter came whistling and the wild cat was frantic. The rat was happy seeing the hunter. Then it immediately cut the net enough for the wild cat to escape and both ran for their lives.

The rat got into the hole again and the wild cat ran away from the sight of the hunter. The baby rat asked its mother, 'You honoured your word and the wild cat also promised to honour its word, why then this drama?.' The rat replied, 'I am not an idiot like your father; that is why I ran. Basically people rarely change their nature. Hence, I had to be alert. '

One must help one's enemy. One should know how to use one's enemy. One must honour one's word and at the same time create a distance from one's enemy.

Thus the rat employed the above wisdom.

DON'T MAKE LIFE INTO A LIFE SENTENCE

Life is not a word. It is a sentence. Please do not make it a life sentence. To live life is to be related and every relationship involves three aspects –

- Relater
- Related
- Relationship

When a relationship is harmonious, life is harmonious and vice-versa. The art of harmoniously relating to life is what religion teaches us.

A villager visited a friend's house. His friend, being an electrical engineer used to experiment with electrical equipments in a room. Every time the villager touched those equipments, he used to get electric shocks. He felt as though a ghost must have been residing in them. Later, his friend taught him how to use those equipments. The villager found to surprise the same room, which was like hell had turned into heaven.

In the same way, the world is like an electrical room. If you relate wisely, it will be a heaven or else the world will be a hell. Lord Buddha used to say 'Mind is a hell; Mind is a heaven.'

Mullah Nazaruddin told his Guru, 'I often get drunk being in bad company. The sad part is that they are all your students who are not practising what you have taught.'

'What did they not practise?' asked the Guru.

'You have taught your students the value of sharing. When I brought alcohol, none of them shared with me and I had to drink alone' cried Mullah Nazaruddin.

Ego has its justifying logic. The logic of the ego is crippling; not freeing. Religion should free us. In the name of religion people are crippled. The true quality of religion is to free oneself.

Once we are ego-less, the joy opens up spontaneously. 'Egolessness' awakens intelligence whereas ego gathers knowledge.

What should one's fundamental attitude be towards a relationship?

The fundamental attitude that one has to have is to change the way we look at problems. Problems do not hurt us but it is how we interpret a problem that hurts us. Only a dead person does not have any problems. To be alive involves living with problems. If we change the attitude that a problem is not a nuisance but it is an invitation for us to be creative, then the very problem would show us the ingredients of solutions. Our task is to discover them. Then a problem becomes an opportunity to grow. This method is known as 'Golden egg technique.' There is a story of a goose, laying golden eggs. So treat a problem as a golden egg. The outer may be an ordinary shell but there is gold inside. This very attitude will make us enthusiastic about dealing with a problem.

Beware – do not exaggerate a problem or underestimate a problem or be indifferent to a problem. Develop an intuitive eye to see a treasure hidden in a problem. Your task is to get at the treasure and not get blown away by the problem.

Problems in a relationship like marriage would then not lead to suffering. Or else marriage would show up in the form of four rings;

- Engagement Ring
- Wedding Ring
- Suffe-Ring
- Endu-Ring

With right understanding, one can make suffering into sacredness. Hence it is said, 'Attitude creates Altitude.'

As far as I know...
Up to a point... To me

Can you elaborate on the concept of relativity in a spiritual paradigm?

Religious people appear to respect a book that they truly neglect. If one truly respects sacred teaching, it is necessary to practise than merely preach. Then the choice becomes simple; you can either stand up and be counted or lie down and be ignored. It is wiser to act on what you choose rather than say what you choose. Among the beautiful teachings of Jainism is Syat Vaada. If one truly practises, the beauty of it will be revealed as an inner freedom. Syat Vaada says everything is relative and nothing is absolute.

For example, if one is practising Syat Vaada, and hears that a person is stupid, then he will say his stupidity is relative and not absolute. Jain seers spoke of the theory of relativity thousands of years before the western world was aware of it. Syat Vaada can be better understood through a story.

A poor Chinese farmer found a beautiful black horse on his farm. The farmer and his only son were excited to see such a beautiful horse. The King of that place learnt about this wonderful horse and offered a huge sum to buy the horse. The farmer humbly rejected the offer. All the villagers told the farmer that he was stupid in rejecting the offer from the King. The farmer answered 'may be.'

After few days the horse was missing. The villagers once again told the farmer, 'Do you realize you were unwise?' The farmer answered again 'may be.' After a few more days the horse returned with 20 other horses. The villagers now told the farmer, 'You are really wise by not selling the horse.' The farmer again answered 'may be.'

The farmer's only son while training the horses fell down and broke his leg. Meanwhile, a war broke out in China, and all youngsters had to go to war except the farmer's son, as he was not fit. The villagers once again said, 'You are lucky, your only son is saved.' The farmer yet again said 'may be.'

This explains in Syat Vaada the things are relative. If one understands the theory of relativity one will not be a victim of absolutisation. How does one practise this principle in daily life? This insight from the above story reveals a lot on how it can help people in their lives. When an opinion is made of a person, the question to be asked is – 'Is it absolute or relative?' Whenever one makes an opinion of others and considers it as absolute, then one stops seeing the person as a flowing being. Nobody is static, everyone is a flowing being. Considering as absolute is, destroying the basic quality of an individual as a flowing being.

How does this concept help in our daily lives?

Syat Vaada involves applying it in the following ways in our daily lives:

- As far as I know
- Up to a point
- To me

The quality of our life depends on the quality of our relationships. Keeping the perception of our relationship relative is keeping it open. Being open gives ventilation to life.

If some one says Mr. X is stupid, then he is not practising Syat Vaada. But if he says, 'As far as I know, Mr. X is stupid,' then he is not labelling the person and at the same time validating his perception, yet being open to other variables which do not make the other person stupid.

So often, we are prisoners of our own knowledge. So by saying, *as far as I know*, I am not making my knowledge as absolute and at the same time not deleting whatever I know and being open to other variables. In this process, I am setting myself free and others free by not labelling the other. We label others and see only the labels and not the persons. This is an ignorant way of living. Jainism tells us to live a life based on this principle and be wise. A wise person creates happiness around and an unwise one creates unhappiness.

Practising Syat means *'up to a point.'* If I can make statements like 'up to a point this person is bad,' then I am allowing myself to see beyond my limiting perception. Any person is bad up to a point. Even a thief is bad up to a point, but he will do good acts for someone he cares for. So how can we say that the thief is bad in absolute terms?

This principle can be applied as *'To me.'* In our perceptions and in our opinions of others, if we tell ourselves that 'To me' a person is bad and not that he is bad in the absolute term. Such a perception is more factual.

We suffer in life for we make absolute statements of others and ourselves. We can set ourselves free and others by practising this principle, which says *maybe* or *things are relative*. When we operate on a relative plane, we are open to other possibilities. Creativity happens in the space of openness.

When we are open, we see opportunities. There are far more opportunities than we think. When opportunity knocks, a wise person is open to the opportunities, whereas an unwise person complains. So openness is a great virtue and this is the result of the practise of the principle – Syat Vaada.

A section of large crowd during Gita Talks by Swamiji

A view of Nirguna Mandir at Bangalore

51, Ground Floor, 16th Cross,
Between 6th & 8th Main
Malleswaram, Bangalore 560 003, India
Tel: +91 80 23444112, 4153 5831-32
Fax: +91 80 4153 5833
E-Mail: prasannatrust@vsnl.com
www.swamisukhabodhananda.org

Prasanna Trust is a registered social charitable trust set up with the objective to re-look at various facets of Indian philosophy and culture for effective transformation of individuals in particular and the society in general.

We have made our presence primarily through :

- Transformative Education
- Social Oriented Service

TRANSFORMATIVE EDUCATION

a) LIFE – LIVING IN FREEDOM – AN ENQUIRY

It is a 2 days workshop on personal effectiveness through interactions and meditations. An experience oriented, non-religious program designed to enhance productivity, handling stress, personal well-being and organisational synergy. It focuses on bringing forth the outer winner leading to creativity and an inner winner to meditative consciousness.

b) EXISTENTIAL LABORATORY

It is a 4-days residential retreat set amidst natural surroundings to experience oneself through a series of dynamic and passive meditations in order to see connectivity with nature, to heal and release the inner child, to realise innocence and wonderment in all walks of life based on the Upanishad truths - Chakshumathi Vidya.

c) CORPORATE HARMONY AND CREATIVITY

It is a 2 days comprehensive workshop for senior level executives to harness creativity and harmony in today's competitive work environment and preparing them for globalisation.

d) YOUTH PROGRAMME

It is a 3 days program based on multiple intelligence. The program develops the hidden talent and skill in a child; to enable the child to face the world with confidence as each child is unique.

e) OH, MIND RELAX PLEASE!

It is a 1 day seminar based on unique techniques to transform from ordinary to extra-ordinary, dealing with fear and conflicts and converting them as challenges..

f) RELATIONSHIP SEMINAR

An exclusive workshop for couples, so as to discover intimacy and togetherness in a relationship.

g) TEACHERS' TRAINING PROGRAMME

A 5 days workshop designed to train and develop an individual as Pracharak or teacher for spreading the universal message for the benefit of society.

h) MANTRA YOGA PROGRAMME – A Holistic approach to Life

A workshop based on five powerful Mantras to help in enhancing health, unlocking the blissful centre, increasing intuitive ability, creating wealth and divinity in oneself and others. This program is conducted in English and also in many Indian languages by well trained Pracharaks.

i) NIRGUNA MANDIR – A Meditation Centre for Learning

* Unfolding the traditional texts of the Bhagavad Gita & the Upanishads as is relevant in today's living context.
* Workshops to bring forth creativity and awareness among youth, women and parents through a spiritual paradigm.
* Research to foster universal love through an inter-religious forum.
* Orientation programs for trainers and social workers.
* Spiritual inputs to deal with phobia, fear, trauma, drug and alcoholic abuse.

SOCIAL ORIENTED SERVICE

a) CHILD CARE CENTRE - A HOME FOR HOMELESS - PRASANNA JYOTHI:

Nurturing lives of little angels who have been orphaned due to the paradox of circumstances. Uncared girls who otherwise would have withered away are growing into enthusiastic, intelligent, celebrative and responsible children.

b) VOCATIONAL TRAINING FOR CHILDREN:

In order to keep abreast with the fast changing face of the world, it is proposed to give the children of Prasanna Jyothi training in office automation & allied area of skills.

We seek support of individuals, business houses, institutions and invite them to be part of this noble vision of creating an atmosphere to impart our culture and thus contributing to the society we build.

Contribution to ***Prasanna Trust*** *account is exempted from* ***Income Tax under Section 80 (G)***

TITLES OF SWAMIJI'S WORKS

BOOKS

Meditation *(from Bhagavad Gita) (also in Tamil & Telugu)*
Karma Yoga *(based on Bhagavad Gita)*
Wisdom through Silence
(Commentary on Dhakshina Murthy Stotram)
Oh, Life Relax Please!
(also in Hindi, Tamil, Telugu, Gujarati and Marati)
Oh, Mind Relax Please!
(also in Tamil, Telugu, Kannada, Malayalam, Hindi, Marati & Gujarati)
Oh, Mind Relax Please! Vol. 2
(only in Tamil, Kannada & Telugu)
Looking Life Differently *(also in Tamil)*
Wordless Wisdom
Stress Management – A bullet proof Yogic Approach
Art of Wise Parenting
Agame Relax Please! *(in Tamil)*
Kutumbave Relax Please! *(in Kannada & Telugu)*

AUDIO
TRADITIONAL UNFOLDMENT

Gayatri Mantra *(also in regional languages)*
Maha Mruthyunjaya Mantra *(also in regional languages)*
Om Gam Ganapate Namaha *(also in regional languages)*
Om Krishnaya Namaha *(also in regional languages)*
Om Shivaya Namaha *(also in regional languages)*
Mantra Chants
Trataka Yogic Technique
Shiva Sutras
Essence of Bhagavad Gita
Guru Purnima

MEDITATION

Brahmayagna
Navratri Upasana
Bhakti Yoga
Mantra Healing
Maha Visarjana Kriya
Meditation, the Music of Silence
Vedic Vision to Pregnant women
Yoga Laya

OCCULT TEACHINGS

Seven Chakras of Hindu Psychology
Symbolism of Hindu Rituals
Essence of Hinduism
Who am I?
Healing Hurt through Gayatri Mantra
Handling insecurity through Mruthyunjaya Mantra
Handling crisis through Taraka Mantra

MANAGEMENT – A NEW LOOK THROUGH SPIRITUAL PARADIGM

Self Confidence through Hypnosis
Stress Management
Art of Parenting
People Management – an enlightened approach
Creating a Happy Marriage
Hypnosis and Relationship
Living in Freedom – an Enquiry
LIFE series

VIDEO (in VCD form)

Suffering to Surrender
Jokes to Joy – Navarasa
Discouragement to Encouragement
Worry to Wisdom
Stress Management through Spirituality
Seeds of Wisdom
Looking Life Differntly
A Balanced Man
Vedanta – the dynamics of living
Inner Awakening
Harmony in Chaos
Bhagavad Gita – Chapter II (Vol. 1, 2, 3 & 4)

Swamiji's workshop empowers one to be Effective, Creative & Celebrative in all walks of life.

'LIFE' - a two-days workshop on how to use the mind for Success and Satisfaction

Objective of the Seminar:

Outer Winner

- The art of powerful goal setting.
- Decision-making, Team building.
- Divine principles of worldly achievement.
- Interpersonal skills & Effective communication
- How to deal with difficult people.
- Possibility thinker.

Inner Winner

- The art of being blissful, restful and loving.
- The art of healing psychological wounds.
- Mind management
- Worry management.
- Fear management.
- Meditation to bring about healthy inner healing and enlightenment.

What others say about the programme:

"Here's one Guru who's in tune with modern times."

– India Today.

"The unusual Swami from Bangalore is the latest Guru on the Indian Management scene."

– Business India.

"He has come to be hailed as the 'Corporate Guru'. The Management Swami has attempted to infuse the Corporate World with the much needed dose of ethics and spirituality."

– The Hindu.

For more details on Swamiji's in-house & public workshops, contact:

PRASANNA TRUST

51, Ground Floor, 16th Cross,
Between 6th & 8th Main
Malleswaram, Bangalore 560 003, India
Tel: +91 80 23444112, 4153 5831-32, Fax: +91 80 4153 5833
E-mail – prasannatrust@vsnl.com
prmadhav@vsnl.com
Visit us at www.swamisukhabodhananda.org

NIRGUNA MANDIR

#1, Nirguna Mandir Layout,
Near I Block Park, Koramangala,
Bangalore – 560 047, INDIA
Phone: (080) 2552 6102

At USA

E-mail: toshakila@hotmail.com
aruna@knology.net
parvathykancherla@yahoo.com

------- ✂ --------------- ✂ -------

Please send me information on

- ☐ **Seminar on LIFE program**
- ☐ **Seminar on Oh, Mind Relax Please!**
- ☐ **Seminar on Corporate Harmony & Creativity at work**
- ☐ **Books, Audio Cassettes, CD's, VCD's**

Name .... Title............................

Company ....

Address ....

....

City .... State.................................... Pin..................

Telephone (Off) .... (Res)..

Fax .... Email...